**LESSONS ON LOVE
AND LIFE LEARNED THE HARD WAY**

Never Make
the Same
Mistake Twice

Nene Leakes
with *Denene Millner*

A Touchstone Book

Published by Simon & Schuster

New York London Toronto Sydney

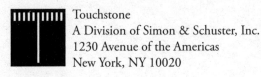

Touchstone
A Division of Simon & Schuster, Inc.
1230 Avenue of the Americas
New York, NY 10020

First Touchstone hardcover edition August 2009

TOUCHSTONE and colophon are registered trademarks of
Simon & Schuster, Inc.

For information about special discounts for bulk purchases,
please contact Simon & Schuster Special Sales at 1-866-506-1949
or business@simonandschuster.com.

The Simon & Schuster Speakers Bureau can bring authors to your live
event. For more information or to book an event contact the
Simon & Schuster Speakers Bureau at 1-866-248-3049
or visit our website at www.simonspeakers.com.

Designed by Aline C. Pace

Manufactured in the United States of America

10 9 8 7 6 5 4 3 2 1

Library of Congress Cataloging-in-Publication Data
Leakes, Nene.
   Never make the same mistake twice : lessons on love and life learned
the hard way / Nene Leakes with Denene Millner.
      p.   cm.
   1. Leakes, Nene.   2. Television personalities—United States—
Biography.   I. Title.
PN1992.4.L36 A3   2009
791.4502'8092 B—dc22   2009018718

ISBN 978-1-4391-6730-4
ISBN 978-1-4391-6732-8 (ebook)

For my sons, Bryson and Brentt,
who are my biggest blessings

Contents

Contents

Never Make
the Same
Mistake Twice

Chapter 1

I AM LARGER THAN LIFE—AND REFUSE TO MAKE APOLOGIES FOR IT

Go to Athens, Georgia, right now, and people will tell you in a heartbeat: Nene hasn't changed one bit. I've always been loud, a little brash, unapologetically truthful, and, above all else, real. I'm like Simon Cowell on *American Idol*: If you say something I don't like, I might as well correct your ass. It's my opinion, and there's nothing wrong with having one. I have, at least, the right to express it, don't I?

And I love expressing it on *The Real Housewives of Atlanta*—in the spotlight. What, you didn't know? I was meant to be in the spotlight. I knew this from the time I was a little girl, trust. I was *that* girl, honey. I would be at home, at my aunt's house, playing with my Barbie in her little pool and my Candi doll, too—you know, the one with the hair and the makeup and the rollers—having loud conversations with the two of them about how Janet Jackson, who was then starring as Penny on *Good Times*, didn't have nothing on me. I'd be doing their hair and getting their makeup right and baking cakes in my Easy-Bake oven and having parties for them and me, just bragging to them and the four walls about how we were all going to go big-time and how my Easy-Bake needed 100 watts because we needed to go big with it. Be clear: My people were sharp, honey. My dolls and I would all be in there looking fierce and I'd be just going on and on about how I was going to be a star, for real. My friends and I would be over there on Dearing Street, hopscotching and playing baseball—the tree was first base, a shoe was second, and a piece of cardboard, third—and we'd be getting down, me talking smack the whole time. If I got my hands on a piece of chalk? Oh, it'd be over. I'd plop right there in the middle of the street and write "Nene" in big bubble letters in different colors, just like I intended to see it up in lights, punctuating each letter I drew with, "I'm going to be famous, y'all. I don't know when this shit is gonna pop off, but I'm gonna be ready when it hits!"

My aunt and everyone else thought I was just a trip. They'd bust into the bathroom and see me in the mirror, posing like that picture of Janet Jackson—the one where she's smiling all cute with her hand behind her head—and crack up laughing at me. They just didn't know where I got all that big personality from, where I got it in my mind that I was going to be a celebrity. But I knew all along I was destined for greatness, and that greatness wasn't about to be found in the old dirt roads of Athens. I was raised on the outskirts of Athens, a cute but small college town in north Georgia. My aunt built her a nice house there—though it looks small today, it seemed huge when I was a kid—but we didn't have even the simplest things everybody had in town. Like cable and paved streets. You could wash your car and spit-shine the tires and then drive down the road leading to my aunt's house and it would seem like your car hadn't seen water since it left the dealership lot. And don't even get me started on how we couldn't watch any good shows on TV. Lord, I couldn't stand being out there with no channels, moving those damn rabbit ears to try to get reception so I could watch something decent. That just wasn't any way for a future star to live.

Besides, I saw early on that Athens did something to people—made them settle for that small-town life and a small-town way of thinking. I watched all my friends and their brothers and sisters, too, graduate from school and then start working at the plant almost the day after they crossed the stage. It didn't seem like it ever occurred to them that the world was so much bigger than our little corner of Georgia, that there were bigger, better opportunities out there. But I had big dreams, and they would reveal themselves in Technicolor and with clear Dolby sound. I was going to be a model, and act, and have money, and a man who was about something. And everything I did was geared toward making my colorful, loud dreams a reality.

I convinced my aunt to let me live with her daughter so that I could go to the school in the city of Athens and so that I could join both modeling school and an acting class downtown. I was on the basketball team and the cheerleading team, and you could usually find me holding court in the restaurants and boutiques in the cute little downtown area near the University of Georgia, the college that anchored Athens. My friends would just watch me move and goad me on. They knew I was a go-getter—a hustler—and that I wasn't hardly studying staying there in Athens the rest of my life. I wouldn't even date a dude from Athens. My girls would date those country guys from in town, and I would be somewhere bragging about the guy I was dating from Oglethorp or the boy who was driving in from Atlanta to visit. And while I was waiting for him to show up? I'd be talking about making it big. Oh, I was a celebrity already in my own mind—was always like, "I don't know what's wrong with the rest of these people, but they better recognize: Nene is a star!"

Now, it didn't pop off like I planned until much later in my life. I got sidetracked with a no-good man who abused me, and then became a young single mom, and after that wound up doing some not-so-popular things to survive, things I'll talk about later in the book. But I never forgot the dream, never lost sight of my vision. I'd find my way to auditions here and there, and eventually ended up meeting the casting director Robbie Reed-Humes, who'd gotten her start casting Spike Lee's earlier films and was enjoying a smoking hot career as *the* person booking talent for the hottest black movies on the big screen. When I met her, I'd been looking for a speaking part in a film so that I could get my Screen Actors Guild card, and Robbie was casting *The Fighting Temptations*, the flick about a secular music producer who agrees to direct a church choir in order to get his inheritance. She got me in front of the director, and he liked me enough to bring me back for a second audition the next day.

Still, because I didn't have a name, I didn't get any of the big parts. Instead, they gave me a bit as a stripper auditioning for the choir. I had on a shirt and jeans, and I had to go up in front of Cuba Gooding's character and take off my top while I tried to convince him I was just perfect for his church group. My scene ended up on the cutting room floor, but I did get that SAG card, which led to me landing a guest starring role on *The Parkers*, and I even auditioned for a lead role in *Girlfriends*—opportunities that kept opening doors for me. I also landed the lead role in *A Time to Dance*, a theater show in Atlanta. My agent even got me a meeting with the head of casting over at UPN. I wasn't on my game in that interview, though. I thought it was an audition and so I showed up in the standard audition outfit of jeans and flip-flops, ready to read and take a head shot and leave my callback information and be on my way. I must have looked so new to her, like I didn't know what I was doing. I'm not going to lie: I didn't. I had no clue that she wanted to talk to me about a new TV show the network was planning—*Eve*—and they were thinking about me as a sidekick. That lady saw my inexperience, but she kept talking to me, and her words inspired me. I learned the lingo from her and got some ideas, too, namely, that a reality show might be the perfect platform for Nene to go big.

I could have gone on *Survivor* or *Big Brother* or the *Flavor of Love*, but none of them felt right, none of them spoke to me. But when a producer came knocking on my door, talking about *The Real Housewives of Atlanta*?

Yeah, it was on.

ON THE REAL

I was a fan of *The Real Housewives of Orange County*—loved those evil bitches calling each other friends and slicing each other up while they smiled and partied together. I thought it was delicious, and it reminded me a lot of the crazy experiences I was having as a wife, a mom, a friend, and some women's worst nightmare right here in the black Mecca—Atlanta. Honey, you couldn't tell me that the drama between me and my girls wasn't as interesting and nutty and off the chain as the mess the Orange County housewives were tossing at my screen every week.

And then, sure enough, I got the phone call.

A friend of mine was talking about how Bravo's *Real Housewives* franchise was trying to set up shop here in Atlanta and they were looking to cast African-American women who "live behind a gate," meaning they had to be wealthy, in the spotlight, and definitely in the know when it comes to what's popping in the ATL. I didn't believe her at first; she's always trying to act like she's so connected and whatnot, so I just said, "Whatever," and kept it moving.

A few days later, though, I got a call from a woman who was out here looking for people to interview. She'd gotten my phone number from my girl and wanted to know if she could stop by to ask me a few questions on camera—you know, to see if I had the right look and feel she and the producers of the show were looking for. She made clear that because they hadn't gotten the green light from Bravo, nothing was assured or guaranteed, even if she got me on camera and thought I was the greatest thing since sliced bread. Now, I was on the other line running my mouth when she called, and honestly, what she was saying sounded a lot like, "I'm going to come to your house, talk to you like you're my best friend for an hour or two, and then go on about my business like we never met," so I was like, "Let me get your number and call you back." After I finished taking my time wrapping up my conversation, I called the woman back and let her talk me into inviting her to come by the house the next day.

Mind you, I still hadn't processed what was about to happen some two hours before she was supposed to be over to the house. I had a lot of stuff going on—there was shopping to be done, and I had a couple of things going on at my younger son's school, and my husband, Gregg, and I had a few things bubbling with our businesses, and frankly, I didn't feel like going above and beyond for this woman. When she showed up to the house with her cameraman and assistant, I was still in flip-flops, camouflage pants, and a wife-beater, hungry because I hadn't eaten and a little lifted because I'd had almost an entire bottle of wine on an empty stomach, you know, to loosen up. Needless to say, when she walked into my house, I was a little loopy, talking about "Heeeeeey! Girl, come on in here!" Being all loud and whatnot.

Typical Nene.

We just got to gabbing and I got to saying all kinds of stuff to her, and somewhere in the middle of all the action, Gregg, who was on my last good nerve at the moment because of a disagreement we'd had earlier, said something to me and I got really smart with his ass. When I figure out how to ask my inebriated self just what the hell I said to him, I'll let you know, but my sober self remembers clearly that the minute I took a bite out of my husband is the minute I could see in the woman's eyes that she liked me for the show. She kept insisting that she couldn't make any decisions until she passed the tape on to someone else to review, but I knew before the door closed behind her that I was in the mix, for sure.

Finally, I was getting my chance to shine.

I PUT 'EM IN THEIR PLACE

I knew *The Real Housewives of Atlanta* was going to be a big deal, but I didn't realize it was going to be *this* big a deal. The first season ended up being the biggest freshman series for Bravo since *Queer Eye for the Straight Guy,* and everybody was talking about it—even CNN's Anderson Cooper, who called me his "favorite" housewife. (For the record: That gray fox could definitely come visit my henhouse anytime!) What most surprised everybody, though, was how the viewers latched on to my tell-it-like-it-is-put-'em-in-their-place straight talk. That was just Nene being Nene. I can sit back and let you get your licks in, but you're not about to push my buttons and take me all the way there without me putting five on it. I really don't care who's around—I was dead serious when I said that I *will* put you in your place. That doesn't mean I'm not a good person, because I am. I have a really big heart and my friends will tell you that I'm as sweet as can be. I don't set out to hurt anyone. I know the difference between telling it like it is and getting smart and making somebody feel bad, and I never set out to make someone feel bad when I'm speaking my mind.

Most times, I do recognize that there's a right and wrong time to speak up, and times when you need to bite your tongue and keep your thoughts to yourself. So I think that above all things, my *Real Housewives of Atlanta* fans appreciated that when I was on their TVs, in their living rooms, the one thing they could count on was Nene being genuine and real. They could tell that I knew when to bite my tongue and when it was time to speak up, and I think they could tell and were proud of the fact that I was being genuine, being who I am. I don't put on airs, I don't boast or brag. I don't see the need for it. My personality is about being outgoing and real—being plain ol' fabulous Nene.

My genuineness came across, and that's why I get love from the people. They can see that I'm just a real girl, a regular chick. I'm not trying to die in Dior or wear Dolce & Gabbana to my funeral. I'm not trying to keep up with the Joneses, either. I was dead serious when I said, "I *am* the Joneses." I drive that nice car. I have the fly husband. I live in the big house. I carry the best handbags and rock the baddest shoes. It's what I do anyway. Why would I try to keep up with you? I'm the girl you are and the girl you're trying to be, all mixed up in one. I'm the one with no makeup on, going out to dinner, getting tore the hell up, singing songs in the car—being real. The clever one who speaks her mind and tells it like it is.

I'm empowered.

I'm self-made.

I know where I came from.

And I know exactly where I intend to go.

THIS I KNOW FOR SURE

Being persistent pays off, that's for sure. I'd always known I would have an incredible platform to showcase my talents, and after years of going on auditions, strutting the catwalk as a model, and even scoring a role in a big-screen motion picture, I was on my way. Maybe the people around me couldn't see it, but I could see it for myself, and I truly believe that my unrelenting desire to be something more than what others envisioned for me helped push me further than anyone could have possibly imagined. It takes a strong person to overcome the adversity I've experienced in my lifetime; coming through those fires wasn't easy, I'll tell you that much. Some days, it felt like I was in the middle of a damn inferno. But always, in the back of my mind, I knew that I was bigger than it all—more fabulous, too. I knew what I wanted, and I wasn't about to let anything get in the way of me being what I wanted to be.

While persistence had a lot to do with my getting my dream gig, I know that being myself took me straight to the top. I'm one of the most popular housewives of the *Housewives* franchise—across all ages, across all races, across both sexes. I've got a Bravo A-List Award to prove it; I took top honors as "Reality's Guiltiest Pleasure," up against Bret Michaels of *Rock of Love*, Kim Kardashian of *Keeping Up with the Kardashians*, Kendra Wilkinson of *The Girls Next Door*, and Gretchen Rossi of *The Real Housewives of Orange County*. And I'll tell you this much: I deserved it. I gave a decent acceptance speech, but what I really should have said was this: "I want to thank all the fake people, because here's what keeping it real will do for you." Some of the people on these shows are wearing the best designer clothes and faking the funk thinking people will like them more, and I didn't do any of that and *still* walked away with the award.

Every last one of my fans has said they tuned in to the show because they knew I was going to say out loud exactly what everyone else was thinking—maybe even with a little more attitude than most. Don't believe me? Check the blogs. Everybody else does, and every now and again they cough up something true. More important, I think fans of the show appreciated that I was just being me; my personality, who I am and how I roll, was clear from the first moment they heard my voice. It's really easy for people to completely switch up who they are once those cameras are on—you might get shy, you might be uncomfortable expressing your opinion, or you might take on the characteristics of someone who, when the cameras are off, you wouldn't dream of being in front of people who know you intimately. All of a sudden it's like, who are *you* right now? People get to tripping and start getting manipulative and ratchet up all kinds of needless drama, all in the name of getting their shine on. They're trying to be someone they're absolutely not, and the viewers—the fans—can tell who they are. But they can also tell who is being genuine, and they're going to go hard for that person—root for her, pray for her, and wish her well.

That's the reward I got for being Nene, for being real on a reality show. I appreciate the love and the support, and I made a point of letting anyone within the sound of my voice know it, too. And some people—specifically a couple of the housewives of Orange County—got a little pissy about that. Okay, a lot pissy about it. And yup, I raise my hand and cop to the fact that I got them all hot and bothered with my bragging.

See, we'd all been at rehearsals for the A-List Awards literally all day, and doing different events in between, and by the time the evening rolled around, we were all dead tired and hungry and in need of a good drink. Vicki Gunvalson, an Orange County housewife, told her fellow cast mates, a few girls from the New York housewives, and me, Sheree, and Lisa that she had reservations for ten at a beautiful rooftop sushi restaurant, and that we were welcome to accompany them to the spot. Vicki and her crew headed on over, and the Atlanta housewives ran back to the hotel for a quick minute, then went on over to the restaurant (Lisa didn't go, but Candy did)—only to find that Vicki's table for ten had no room for us. They'd filled up all the extra seats with people we didn't even know, and what's worse is that while we were standing there trying to figure out why those heiffas didn't make good on our seats, only a few of them bothered to open their mouths to speak to us!

When I tell you we didn't pay them any mind, I mean we didn't pay them any mind, just sashayed our cute asses right behind the hostess on over to the couch while she had someone prepare a table for us. We waited for about twenty minutes for a table right up against a wall overlooking their restaurant and, specifically, the Orange County housewives' soiree. But our attention was on us—our conversation and laughter came easily as we recalled the day's events and looked forward to the awards ceremony. While we were kickin' it, Orange County housewife Tamra Barney and her husband came over to the table to say hello—the only two at the entire table to show a little class and at least come over and speak. But she didn't come empty-handed. She had dirt on Kim, who apparently had been running all around town saying all kinds of foul stuff about us. When she finally wrapped up her story, I just looked at her and said, "Y'all are a trip. Vicki and Jeana [Keough, another OC housewife] are not being friendly."

Tamra didn't say anything, just stared. And I kept going. "But anyway, I don't care what you say—the Atlanta housewives put the *Housewives* franchise on the map!"

Whoo—what did I say *that* for? Tamra let out a nervous laugh. "You know Vicki and Jeana are going to kill you for saying that!"

"Oh, no, the hell they're not." I sniffed. "Run on over there and tell them I said it."

Well, Tamra walked her ass back to the table, my eyes following her all the way over to my nemeses and then training on the three while Tamra let my words rush through her lips. She must have been making it really juicy, too, because all I could see was Vicki and Jeana leaning in and shaking their heads and their mouths falling agape, like someone had just told them the most tragic news. And quick as a wink, Vicki headed back to our table; steam practically rose from her blond dye job, she was so damn pissed. And when she stomped up to the table, I put a big ol' grin on my face, waved my hand, and gave her a cheery, "Heeeeey!"

Vicki didn't bother with niceties—she just laid right into my ass. "Don't even try it, Nene. I paved the way for the Atlanta housewives!" she insisted, shaking her head.

"You may have paved the way, but the Atlanta housewives put the *Housewives* franchise on the map," I said smugly, still smiling.

"Oh, no you didn't!" she said, clearly not amused.

"Yes we did," I continued matter-of-factly, getting her even more heated.

When she finally saw that I wasn't budging, she changed the subject and started talking about her insurance company or something, and then she turned her attention to my husband, Gregg. He was interested in the insurance business so Vicki gave him some advice, and then she was on her way.

Oh, it was just perfect. I knew Tamra would be the perfect one to spread the word. I'd been looking for someone all day to take that message back to Vicki, knowing full well she'd blow a damn gasket. I mean, those girls are some hateful bitches—mean and impossible to work with. Same for a few of the New York girls. In fact, Ramona Singer from *The Real Housewives of New York* almost caught it that same week when we were all in the green room waiting to go on to our next function, and I was midsentence talking about something or other, and she just yelled out to me, "Shut up!" Like she'd lost her damn mind. "I'm hungry and I'm ready to go and you guys are talking and I just want you to shut up!" she whined.

"Oh, you better hold on, Ramona," I snapped. "Somebody better tell those chicks from New York that shit is *not* about to happen up in here!"

I don't know if she temporarily lost her damn mind, but I wasn't about to stand there and let her tell me to shut up, like I'm some child. I mean, those girls from the other shows would have me ready to box on the regular. I told Bravo that if they really wanted a good show, they should have all of us live together. Now *that* would be a trip.

But whatever—can't none of them hold a candle to my

shine. I meant it when I said it: *The Real Housewives of Atlanta* did put those other shows on the map, and if we're going to tell the truth about it, we might as well go on ahead and give me my props for keeping it interesting.

And you best believe, the fun has just begun.

Chapter 2

I'M A CELEBRITY, BUT I AIN'T NO JOKE

Let's see: I'm cheating on my husband with Wesley Snipes. Which is a good thing, considering my husband and I got kicked out of our $800,000 home. I'm not quite sure yet where to stash my stolen flat-screen TVs, though. Seeing as I'm broke, I'm not quite sure where I'll be living either, and if I don't have a house, I don't have a wall to hang the stolen flat-screens. But I'll be sure to let the gossip wags know when I get a house and a wall to hang the TVs on; I intend to position one right above the bed Wesley and I will sleep in. We could take turns watching each other on television after we make mad, passionate love and plot and plan the next electronics store heist.

Sound ridiculous?

Maybe because it is. Every bit as stupid as all of this sounds, this is only some of the stuff I found recently when I googled my name. Some of my celebrity girlfriends warned me early in the taping of the first season of *Real Housewives* that the mess would fly once people started watching the show, and I figured there would be some untruthful things circulating. After all, I'd lived through the madness with my friend Diana, a woman with whom I'd gotten close after she auditioned for *The Real Housewives of Atlanta*. She didn't make it onto the show, but we'd talked during the interviewing process, kept in touch, and went on to become fast friends. Anyway, I'd watched Diana's child support case get scrutinized practically line by line on the blogs—most of it ridiculous, and a lot of it casting her in a negative light. But I didn't know it would be this crazy. In fact, it took me a minute to figure out what, exactly, was being said about me. I'm not computer savvy, and up until just after the show came out, I didn't even know what a blog was. But my friends told me to google my name, and I did it, and I was like, "Wow." But this crap right here? I did not see coming.

For sure, I've always dreamed of being a big enough star for people to want to write and talk about me, but I didn't expect the rumors and innuendo to be this nasty. My name showed up on blogs with all kinds of crazy stories being written about me, and when I scrolled down to the comments, it was even worse. They were getting flip in the lip about my hair, my boobs, my height, my marriage, my kids, my extended family, my daddy, my hometown, the brand of car I drive, my attitude, my voice, my education, my house and mortgage, my neighbor-hood, my wallet, my husband's wallet, his businesses, my foundation, what I've done for a living in my past, what I do for a living now, what I do for fun, what I said about who, and more. I was called illiterate, ghetto, chicken head, a welfare project chick, evil, ugly, fake, loud, phony, broke—you name it, somebody said it. One blog even claimed to have found "skeletons in my closet," claiming I'd cheated on my husband, and not once but several times.

This kind of stuff is a hard pill to swallow, you know? I'd always dreamed of being famous, and I always knew that my dream would come true one day, and I'd heard through the grapevine that there would be certain things I wouldn't be able to say or do once I got into the public eye because they could come back to haunt me. But the whole gossip part of it, I have to admit, I didn't really think through, didn't consider how my words would be twisted around, or how people would misconstrue and mischaracterize my actions, or just straight make up things about my life and swear on a stack of two Bibles to sweet baby Jesus that they're telling the God's honest truth—or at least the truth as they read it on someone else's damn blog. I'd get mad about the rumors if they weren't so damn dumb. Most of the time, I just let it roll off my shoulders.

Let them wag their tongues.

It only makes me look more fabulous than I already am.

SEARCHING FOR PEACE

I will tell you this, though: I think most celebrities think like I think—that you want to have the celebrity and all the great things that come with it, but you want to be able to live a normal life, too. But celebrity and normal don't go hand in hand, and so life changes. It gets harder.

For instance, I can't just go to Walgreens and pick up a prescription or hit the grocery store to pick up a quart of milk and a pint of ice cream and keep it moving. Somebody—in fact, a lot of somebodies—inevitably stops me and tries to hold a half-hour conversation, or pulls out a camera to take a picture, or just shouts my name out at the top of her lungs so that everybody else within a ten-mile radius knows I'm in the house, too. I've even tried to hit the grocery store in the nighttime, when there're fewer shoppers, but that doesn't work, either. People still stop and talk or stare at me, or follow me down the aisles. They don't understand or care that I might not be feeling well, or I'm in a rush, or I really would prefer to pick out tampons without an audience, or I just don't feel like having a half-hour conversation—again—about Sheree's silly ass or Kim's wig. They may not know that I just had an argument with my husband, or I'm worried about something that happened to one of my sons, or I've got cramps and I just want to get some aspirin and then get back home to my warm bed and a cup of hot tea and sleep it off, without aggravation. I may have been working long days for the past two weeks with no breaks, and this one particular day when you see me may be the first time I've been out without the video cameras and flashing lights tracking my every move.

I don't feel obligated to explain any of this to anybody. But I do wish that fans would acknowledge that sometimes I don't feel like talking, dammit. It's nothing personal.

People take it that way, though. Like this chick who almost got checked when Gregg and I went to a restaurant one evening. I had been at home all day, and we didn't have any food in the house and both of us were starving, so we decided on a whim to go get something good to eat at this cute restaurant in Duluth. Now, the place was packed and the line was snaking all out the front entrance, and it was clear that there was going to be a long wait for us to get that plate. That's when celebrity comes in handy. Gregg went and talked to the manager, told him who I was, and within seconds he was calling me in past the crowd to be seated. Check one for celebrity.

But then the whole evening was almost ruined when, as we made our way to our table, a woman grabbed my hand as I walked by and said, "Oh, Nene, what's up?"

I was busy trying to get to that empty table the manager "found" for us, and I didn't want to make a big scene out of the fact that we'd just gotten there and were about to be seated before people who'd been waiting there for close to an hour, so I just said, "Hey," and kept it moving. Well, she said to her girlfriends and loud enough for me to hear, "Oh, no, she didn't! Nene done gone Hollywood."

I know Jesus, and plus I was hungry, so I ignored her butt that time. But when we got settled at our table, she actually came over and accused me of being extra.

"Girl, you were acting like you didn't know who I was," she said, standing over Gregg and me. "It's me!"

I looked at her good this time and kinda realized who

she was: a hairstylist and the mother of the child of a popular
R & B singer. I met her one time when I was in a rush to get my
hair done and went to my girl's salon on the fly. My friend, who
already had a few ladies waiting to get into her chair, told me to
let her coworker curl me right quick, and I did. She did a nice
enough job that day, but not nice enough for me to remember
her like she was family or something. I mean, we never talked
on the phone, we never hung out, we didn't roll in the same circles, nothing. So I was kinda shocked that she was acting like I'd
slapped her mama and stomped her child because I didn't say
hello as enthusiastically as she expected.

Anyway, I acknowledged we'd met before and asked her
how she was doing and secretly hoped she would keep it moving
because I was hungry and didn't feel like chatting. She finally
got the hint and went back over to the bar with her girls, just as
Gregg excused himself to get us a couple of drinks. And wouldn't
you know: She was over there telling her friends, "She's a trip!
I was saying, 'Oh, no, you did *not* act like you don't know who
I am!'"

I had it in my mind to go over there and let her ass have
it, but Gregg, being the wise man that he is, told me to just ig-
nore her because, at the end of the day, she could sit over there
and talk shit all she wanted to. She couldn't stop my bills from
being paid or get me fired from my job or make the sun stop ris-
ing in the morning, so what should I care?

But I *did* care. I can't stand it when people presume to
know me, my family, my history, my business, everything about
me, when they know good and damn well hell they don't, and
then act like I'm the bitch because I don't respond the way *they*
want me to. And besides, isn't it just rude to stand over someone

at a dinner table and talk over her food? I'm not a star-struck person; the only celebrity I've ever approached in my lifetime like that was T.I., and that was only because my baby, Brentt, was going crazy and begging me to take him to meet his favorite rapper. So I did it. And I would do it again for Oprah. But it wouldn't occur to me to pull up a chair to a celebrity's table and hold a meaningless conversation while she and her husband are trying to have intimate time together. (Believe it or not, this has happened to us on several occasions. Once, a woman sat next to us in our booth for so long that Gregg got up pissed and left me sitting there with her while she talked on . . . and on . . . and on . . . for what seemed like an eternity.)

Neither would I think that intimate details of my life would be mischaracterized and then splayed across legitimate news services as if they were fact. This is worse than the most disgusting thing any blogger can say about me and my family because people know that you can't trust the blogs to tell you the truth 100 percent of the time, but what you see on the TV news and in the newspaper is usually investigated in some kind of way and checked and double-checked to make sure it's accurate before it hits the screen and is touted as the gospel.

For sure, it broke my heart to turn on the local news show that I've watched most of my adult life only to have them tear me and my family down and proclaim we'd gotten kicked out of our home for not paying what amounts to practically pennies in rent. The story had some merit to it. We were renting a house, we did go without paying the rent, and we did move out of it—that part the news got right. What they did not tell you was that we'd sold our million-dollar home and were renting in an upscale neighborhood near where our old house was because we liked the area and wanted to keep our son in the same school. What that news report also didn't tell you was that the owner of the house we were renting was getting foreclosure notices because she kept falling behind on her mortgage payments—through no fault of ours. It turns out the bank had sold the mortgage to other companies several times and no one knew. This means payments were going to one place that were meant for another. Now, Gregg and I had our family living in that house, and it seemed like every few months we'd get another notice saying that the house was about to be foreclosed on. We didn't know from one month to the next if someone was going to come by and put our stuff out on the street.

So finally we decided to move, and we refused to pay her another dime in rent because we felt like she wasn't dealing with us in good faith, that it was her neglect to pay the mortgage on time and to the correct place that forced us to move or face getting put out for something we had no control over. She responded to our nonpayment with an eviction notice, and Gregg went to court over it. When he explained to the judge that we were not comfortable paying anymore or even living there anymore, it was agreed upon by my husband and the owner to pull the eviction, apply the deposit, and settle all the difference owed.

Now *that* was the truth. But instead of the truth, what we got was a bunch of innuendo, which led to gossip, with blogs calling for Bravo to change the name of our show to *The Broke Housewives of Atlanta* and questioning my husband's business dealings and trampling all through his personal financial affairs and past relationships.

It was ugly.

And I felt like I was to blame because none of this would have been happening to my husband, and my kids wouldn't have had to endure news reports that they were about to be homeless, if it weren't for me and my success. That was—and still is—the hard part of celebrity.

What's worse is that people spread all kinds of gossip and lies about you, and you have absolutely no control over it. Hell, half the time you don't even know where it comes from. The bloggers and gossipmongers don't have faces or any real way for you to hold them accountable, but at least you can click on "post comment" and give them a bit of the truth. That TV "investigation" into the home Gregg and I shared came, I think, as a result of an anonymous letter about me and mine sent to all of the major Atlanta television stations. Yup, a newscaster I'm associated with called me to break the news. Someone who used an obviously fake name sent a note saying all kinds of terrible things about us—that all the flat-screen TVs in our house were stolen, that we were renting our house for the TV show, and a bunch of other stupid shit that wasn't true and didn't make sense. Renters or not, most people can't afford the monthly rent that we paid, and we lived there before the show was out, so what do any of the lies that person was spreading mean anyway?

I tell you, I was so damn heated behind that, I believe I could have stuck my finger into a pitcher of ice water and made it boil. I had my closest family members and my attorneys in the living room with me, and I was pacing back and forth, trying to decide what to do about it, trying to figure out who could have said such ugly things about me. I don't have any enemies that I know of—at least I didn't then—but it could have easily been a hater I was friends with back in the day, or someone Gregg did business with and it didn't work out, or just some nasty person who didn't know anything about me and mine getting his or her rocks off planting false news with reputable news organizations. And you know what? All but one of those news stations that got the letter threw that worthless piece of paper in the garbage—all of them except the station that decided to treat it like an "anonymous tip" and pursue it like they were gunning for a damn journalism award. I mean, there's so much other shit in the world to report on—kids are being kidnapped and murdered, people are losing their homes to foreclosure for real, men are stealing billions of dollars from old people's retirement funds, and lots more—and you're telling me a reality show star is the biggest news around here?

Uh-huh, okay.

THIS I KNOW FOR SURE

Well, I'll tell you this much: That letter and the fallout behind it hurt my heart, but it didn't break me. You hear that? Trust me when I tell you that Nene is rolling like Mary J. Blige—just fine, fine, fine, fine, fine, fine, whoo! Wag your tongues all you want to, but I'm strong, honey—a hustler. And far from broke. We don't work for free. I get a paycheck like everybody else, and in addition to being a celebrity, I'm a businesswoman; I hire attorneys, I negotiate contracts, and I make deals, baby. I've got four in the works as we speak, and I'm turning down others because I can't fit another thing into my schedule.

Broke?

Don't. Think. So.

Cheating on my husband? Please. Gregg and I have a fantastic relationship—been married and going strong for twelve years, and that's not about to change because some blogger is making up stories about me getting it on with a man I've never even met.

But for all the madness that I deal with as a celebrity, I wouldn't change it for the world. You know why? Because being a celebrity has its perks. I was already in the know when it came to all the best places to party and eat and have a nice time, but now that people know who I am, I have the luxury of not only going to the most fabulous affairs but also being asked to host them, or being paid just to show up and be Nene. That's right: I get invited to the hottest parties, I never have to wait in line, and other stars—from pro football player Terrell Owens to celeb chef and talk show host Rachael Ray—fly me all across the country to have me stand with them. And I enjoy the hell out of that.

I just have to keep reminding myself that Google is my best friend and my worst enemy, that it's best to shake off the haters and to enjoy every minute of my success. Sometimes I fall down, but I ain't ever out the game, baby. Whoever wrote that letter, get ready to write another one, because Nene is here, and she ain't going no damn where. I've been through way too much in my life to let a blog steal my shine, trust that.

Chapter 3

A CHILD SHOULD NEVER BE DENIED
HER MOTHER'S LOVE

To hear my aunts and uncles tell it, I'm exactly like my mom: tall like her, similar facial features, outspoken, and funny as hell. They tell me all the time that she missed her calling, that she could have easily been the female Chris Rock, standing up on a stage somewhere making people fall out in hysterics. I guess I could see how someone could say we're alike, too, especially if you're comparing our personalities and sense of humor. And we both kicked off our twenties as struggling single moms, trying to figure out how to make our marks on the world even in the face of the adversities that came with being young, cash-strapped, and alone.

But that's where our similarities end.

I made a point of doing what I could to *not* be like my mom, especially when it came to the kind of mother I ended up being.

See, my mother left Athens when she was eighteen years old, with nothing but a newborn swaddled tight in baby blankets and a pipe dream about building a life in a new and exciting city with her baby's father—Curtis, her on-again, off-again boyfriend. They didn't live together. He'd joined the military by the time my mother moved to New York with her newborn son—my brother Anthony—into her brother's house in Queens. The next time her shadow darkened a doorway in Athens, she was pregnant again—this time, with me.

So there she was, only about twenty, with two little babies, no real way of making a comfortable life for herself, and trying to keep a long-distance relationship with a man who was in the military and, from what I understand, not at all as into her as she was into him. Needless to say, she was struggling. She was a million miles away from the only home she'd ever known and the only support system—her Georgia-based family—she'd ever had. Alone.

Before long, my aunt tells me, she got a couple of phone calls from people up north—friends and family telling her that my mother was leaving my brother and me at the homes of strangers all around town while she worked or ran the streets or whatever she was doing up there in Queens. And so my aunt—my mother's sister—did what so many grown folk in the black community have done when children were vulnerable and in need of a firm, caring hand: She told my mother to bring Anthony and me to her "just for a little while, until you get back on your feet."

I don't remember much about my life with my mother in Queens. I was really little—only about three years old—when my mother shipped us down to Athens to be raised by our aunt. And then my mom went on with her life, acting, it seemed, as if we'd hardly ever existed. All I know is once we got to Georgia, we didn't ever go back to living with our mother—never knew what it was like to have our own room in her house, or wake up and have her cook breakfast for us before we went to school, or have her tuck us into bed the night before Christmas, telling us we better hurry up and go to sleep if we wanted Santa to leave gifts under the tree, *our* tree.

Instead, we spent our entire childhood living with our aunt, and visiting our mom when it was convenient for her. When my brother and I were really young, we'd go for months without hearing her voice, a year before we would see her face again. Sometimes, her phone number would just stop working, and my aunt would have no way to reach her, to tell her how I was growing, or what my personality was like, or about my accomplishments—or, simply, that I missed her. There were days that I would ask, "Can I call my mom? I wish I could talk to her." My aunt would shoot me a knowing look and then give it to me straight, no chaser: "I tried to call her number, but it's not working," she'd say simply. "I don't know how else to get hold of her, so we have to wait for her to call us."

But the calls would come only sporadically, if at all.

Now, I've been a young single mom, so I understand what it means to have to hustle to provide for your family, to have to spend an enormous amount of time trying to figure out what your game plan is. I'm told that sometimes her phone was disconnected because she couldn't pay the bills. Simply put: She was having a rough time up there in New York, and there wasn't a lot she could do for us down in Georgia.

But even with all the things you can't give your child when you're struggling, the one thing you should always have for the person who has your blood running through her veins is love. Shoot, as long as there were phones available somewhere, she could have found a way to call, no matter if she didn't have a phone where she was staying; as long as the post office sold stamps, she could have gotten one and licked it and put it on an envelope and mailed a quick letter to her kids—"Hey, babies, I miss you and I love you."

We weren't asking for her to mail the moon to us in a Tiffany blue box with a satin bow. We weren't expecting her to dial my aunt's digits everyday at precisely 8:09 P.M., or else we'd refuse her phone call. And while I understand now that it would have been virtually impossible for her to raise us two babies on her own with no help from anybody, I'm figuring that if she truly loved us the way a mother is supposed to love her kids, she would have worked her ass off to get back on her feet so that she could make a stable, loving home for us. With. Her. And if she couldn't provide that, then she could have talked to us, let us know what was going on. That's all I'm saying. All we needed was to hear from her, to have her say, "Look, Mommy doesn't have the money, and the reason you're with your aunt is that

Mommy's life isn't stable right now." It could have been so different—I would have thought so much better of her if there were more conversation, more explanation.

Instead, she simply went on with her life—had more babies; finally gave up on trying to forge a relationship with Curtis, my dad; and married a man who made life extremely comfortable for her and her other kids. Now, you would figure that if she had the money and the means to have all her kids live with her, she would have done this. But nope: She didn't come get us when she got financially stable. Instead, she built a nice life for her family and let my aunt raise us.

SUMMER MOM

When she did see us, it was usually the summertime, when she'd arrange for us to come stay with her while school was out. I was always excited to go to New York. It was the city, and I loved being there—going down to Jamaica Avenue to check out all the latest fashions, and going to Carvel to get soft vanilla ice cream with rainbow sprinkles, and to all those big malls to shop. Mostly, I was just happy to be near my mom because I missed her so.

Still, sometimes it felt more like we were visiting cousins or something, instead of her children. I liked playing with both of my half sisters, but it never felt like we were sisters. It was more like I was a friend coming to spend the summer. We'd play and laugh and do the things that little girls do, and most times we were happy with one another, but we spent so little time together during the course of a year that we never really connected on a sister level. A part of that, for sure, was because of my mom.

See, when we visited her in Queens, and later, at the second home she shared with her husband—my stepdad—in Athens, Anthony and I slept in the guest room, a place that made us feel deep down inside that no matter what, we weren't to get comfortable, ever. That's how it felt to me, at least. Our mother would say stuff that made it crystal clear, too, like when we were playing in my sisters' rooms and our mother came in and said, "Okay, they have to go to bed now so you guys gotta come out of there so they can sleep." I'd be saying to myself, "Well, dang, what are we, visitors? Don't we have to go to bed, too?" She was a mother to them—a grown-up with capabilities to tell them what to do and guide them in the right direction, the way that mothers do. But my brother and I didn't get that kind of care, that attention to details. And even though I was young, I knew the difference. The difference was huge. Or at least it felt like it was.

I remember one time when she came to Athens, to my aunt's house, and brought my two half sisters along for the ride. It was the Fourth of July, and we were all excited about the holiday and hopped up on barbecue and getting ready to go see some fireworks when I noticed my mother in the back room getting my sisters dressed. There was just something about the way she was helping them into their new little outfits and fussing over their hair, making sure it looked just right. I remember standing there, feeling all tall and lanky and odd looking, wishing she put just a little damn effort into helping me get dressed or was concerned about the way my hair looked or standing me at arm's length so that she could admire her handiwork. I mean, I still looked cute and all, but it didn't seem like she was all that concerned about what I looked like, or having any hand in making me—her child—look just as nice as her other girls.

That feeling never went away for me. There was even one day at school when I was crying like a damn baby because all of my friends were getting pumped for the prom and talking about their moms helping them pick out their dresses and their shoes and taking them to get their hair done and their manicures and pedicures, too—you know, making a great big ol' deal about helping their daughters prepare for one of the most important dates of their lives. And all I had to look forward to was getting my whole self ready for my prom by my damn self. I picked out my own dress and the shoes. I did my own makeup and saved up to get my hair done. And when I left my aunt's house with my date, my mother was nowhere to be found—no kiss good-bye, no posing for pictures, no lectures about not letting that little boy I was dating take advantage of me on such a momentous occasion. Nothing. It was as if I were in it alone. As if I didn't have a mother.

She didn't treat me horribly, she didn't have me tied up in the closet, or beat me with a shoe, or torture me or anything like that. But she didn't treat me like I was her child, either. I don't remember her ever telling me that she loved me. If she did say, "I love you" and "I miss you," I sure as hell didn't feel like she did—it simply didn't feel like she really meant it. On the occasions when I did actually see her, she would say "bye" when it was time for me to go and give me a hug that just didn't feel like the kind of hug you give a child you only see once or twice a year.

A MOTHERLESS CHILD

We spent a lifetime like that, with my mother reaching out, it seemed, because she was obligated to, not because she really *wanted* to. My aunt was the one who raised us, paid for our little extracurricular activities, registered us for school, took us to church, bought our clothes, fed us breakfast, lunch, and dinner, disciplined us when we were cutting up, took us to the doctor when we were sick. All of that. Like she'd given birth to me and Anthony herself.

When I got old enough to understand what was going on, and certainly to process my own thoughts and feelings about the situation, I actually asked my aunt why our mother never came to get us. It worried me so. My aunt told me that eventually, she did ask if she could take us back. But by then, my aunt and uncle, who hadn't had a child together, didn't want to give us back to our mom. "We fell in love with you guys, Nene," my aunt said simply. "And so you stayed." For sure, when Anthony and I were in middle school, my aunt backed up those sentiments when she and my uncle formally adopted us. Part of the reason they made our parent/child relationship official was that my uncle, who'd been on disability with a severe work-related back injury that left him unable to walk without assistance, needed some extra cash coming into the house since they were taking care of us without any financial help from our biological parents. He and my aunt would be able to claim us as dependents for a bigger disability check. They made that plain when they sat Anthony and me down to tell us they were putting in papers for us. But my aunt and uncle also made clear that they were adopting us because they loved us, and because we'd been with them most of our lives, and we felt, to them, like we were their own children.

It was a feeling I never experienced with my mother.

When we were older, my mom and her new husband tried to be a part of my life, but really, it was too late for all of that, and our interactions always seemed to turn into some big after-school special drama. Oh, honey, we butted heads, you hear me? My mother and her husband would come down especially hard on me when they were paying attention to what I was doing. Like the time they gave me a brand-new Honda Accord for graduation and then promptly took it away from me and gave it to my brother. Yup, bought me a ride and then took it and gave it away. To this day, I still don't know what I did to deserve that; I just remember being at home and watching my brother speed down the street, the music blasting, looking all fly in *my* damn car. He even drove it to New York from Georgia, put all kinds of miles on it, had his friends all in the passenger seat and backseat, doing goodness knows what in there. Eventually, they gave the car back to me, but by then it didn't feel like mine anymore.

And don't even get me started on the foul things they said to me when I got my first progress reports back from Morris Brown. Now, I admit that I was a less than stellar student. Okay, I'm going to be for real: My grades sucked. I don't know how my aunt found out, but she relayed the bad news back to my mom and stepdad, and they went off on my ass. My stepdad had paid my tuition and room and board, so they had the right to be upset, I guess. But there were way more *f* bombs tumbling from their lips than there was any kind of understanding about why I wasn't doing well in college. They weren't trying to hear about how hard the classes were or what a tough transition it was to go from the rigidity of high school to the freedom of living on my own and keeping my own schedule. They weren't hardly impressed that I was the first runner-up in the Ms. Morris Brown Freshman Court. The only thing they had to add to the conversation besides the cut-to-the-quick cuss-out was a promise that they weren't going to give me a second chance or another dime toward my second year at Morris Brown. "Wasting all our money," my mother yelled into the phone. "You better figure out how to get yourself through school because we're not paying for that shit."

I can only guess that they gave me the car and paid for college because my mom was trying to make up for not raising me. She was quick to take it all back, though, when it turned out that I wasn't perfect. I ended up getting financial aid to get through the next year and got absolutely no help from them. Don't get me wrong: She had every reason to be mad—I get it. She could have sat me down and talked to me, but it just seemed easier for her to check out than to be a parent.

And that lack of a relationship and emotions and feelings definitely seeped into the relationship I have with my half sisters. I never had a sisterly connection with them. It's not their fault or mine; we just weren't together and all three of us have different dads and we just don't see eye to eye on anything.

Over the years, we've had disagreements about everything and nothing—most of it so dumb I can't even remember why we were arguing in the first place—but the result is that we don't talk. At. All. I simply have nothing inside of me that says, "Reconcile, Nene." That may be a part of me that I have to work on, but I just don't have anything in me to see if I can work it out. I've tried over the years and they have, too, I guess, but we're nothing alike and it's been many more years of pain than pleasure with the two of them and so we've had no relationship and I don't see us having one anytime soon.

My mother and I were cordial to one another by the time I reached adulthood. It wasn't like we never talked. We might have had a disagreement and gone for a week without speaking, but we always came out of it on the other side. I remember when I had my baby how excited she was for me, how she was looking forward to meeting her grandson. She wasn't there for his birth—she was in New York and I was down here in Georgia—but I sent her a picture and she called me to say how handsome Bryson was. "Give me that baby," she said, laughing. I promised her in that phone call that she would get to see him soon enough; she said she couldn't wait to meet him.

And within a few months of that phone call, she was gone. My mother died of kidney failure when I was twenty-two and my baby was new. It was a shock to all of us because even though we knew she needed a new kidney, she had been on dialysis for five years and she was doing fine. But she hadn't been following the diet the doctor gave her to keep her body protected. I'm told that every now and then she would eat a piece of cake or a piece of pie and say, "I know I'm not supposed to have this, but I want it." And she would go on ahead and have her cake or her pie, and her body would rebel a little, but she'd always get better and keep waiting on her kidney. Of course, one of us kids probably would have been a perfect match for my mom's organ, but we were all pretty young—the oldest, my brother, was about nineteen when she first started having kidney issues, I was only about seventeen, and our half sisters and brothers were just children. My mom told anyone who would listen that she didn't want any of her babies to give her a kidney, that she would wait on one rather than put her kids through any medical danger. So she just waited. And took care of her body as best she could, except on the days when she needed something sweet.

One day, though, her body gave up on her. She ate something that didn't agree with her and she got sick and needed to get to the hospital stat. My stepfather drove her there. On the way, she laid her head on his shoulder, and by the time he got her to the hospital, she'd slipped into a coma, and then very quickly died after that. It was so shocking and hurtful to my stepdad because he was very much in love with her and, just like that, one evening, she was gone. Even more hurtful was that shortly after she died, maybe a few months later, my stepfather got a call from an organ donor organization, telling him that my mom's name had come up on the list and a kidney was ready for her. They didn't know she'd died.

My stepfather was devastated, he really was. This sweet, caring man had to soldier on without the woman he adored, raising their children alone and clinging to his memories of his wife. He held on to her things in his house for years. He kept all of her clothes and shoes, and the house in Georgia was kept decorated exactly how my mother had laid it out—not a single thing moved. Years later, he brought all my mother's clothes and shoes to Georgia to give to my aunt. But he never remarried.

I can't say that I felt the same way about my mom's death. That's not an easy thing for me to say, but it is what it is. I remember getting the call. I was holding Bryson in my arms in my aunt's bedroom, and my aunt told me that my mother "passed away." I said, "What does that mean, passed away?" I honestly didn't know what it meant. It wasn't like anyone in my life had ever died, you know, so it wasn't something anyone had ever said to me before that very moment.

"She's dead, Nene," my aunt said. "Your mama is dead."

I remember saying, "Oh, my God!" and crying and being sad. But I honestly can say that I wasn't heartbroken. I have friends who've had a parent die and their lives are shattered—they're devastated by it and really have to figure out how to move on from the crushing loss. I never, ever felt like that. I couldn't find the feeling inside me. As much as I wanted to, as hard as I tried, I couldn't mourn her death the way most children mourn the loss of their mother. I knew it wasn't right that she died, and it was shocking, but I wasn't in mourning. It was more like, "Wow, that's my mom and she died." I was sad the way one would be sad if a somewhat distant aunt had died.

The only explanation I have for this is that we weren't close.

And I spent a lifetime trying to figure out why.

Eventually, I would find out, though.

My mom had secrets, some adult mess that seeped all the way into the relationship she had with me.

And there's nothing I can do about any of the mess she's laid at my doorstep—except to make sure that I never do to my children what my mother did to me.

THIS I KNOW FOR SURE

I may not be the best mother in the world, but dammit, I'm the best mother I can be to my boys. My husband, Gregg, says all the time that I spoil our children. I don't know about that; they're not rotten by any stretch. Sure, there are plenty of times when questionable behavior is met with a little more hugging and a lot less discipline than what I got when I was growing up. But I do get on my boys, you can believe that. I'm a screamer— I'll yell my ass off if they step out of line. But I make sure to point out that I'm yelling at them and schooling them, too, because I love them and because I don't want them to make mistakes and have to go through life doing everything the hard way, especially because no adult stepped in and actually parented them or showed them the right way to do things. I didn't have any of this kind of parental guidance from my mom, but I'll be damned if my children aren't going to get that guidance from me. And if I have to drill it into them by being a little loud, well, that's the way it's going to go down. How about that?

But love and hugs and affection will always be mixed up in it. I know what it means to be a child growing up and feeling like your mother doesn't love you. I knew from the moment my first son entered this world that he would experience no greater love than that which he'd get from his mother. It was my sole mission in life to keep my child with me at all times, to do whatever it took so that I would never be in a position where I'd have to leave him with someone while I figured it out. It was also a mission of mine to make sure that he had all of what he needed and some of what he wanted, too, and that those things came from me, exclusively. I would have liked it if his father had just a tiny bit of "act right" in him, but even if his daddy wasn't going to come correct, best believe Nene was going to have her child in nothing but the best. My boys have wanted for nothing, never had a reason to feel envious of anyone else, because their mother has seen to it that they're straight. When Bryson went to his prom, I hooked him up. All the things I wanted my mom to do for me when I was getting ready for the prom, I made sure I did for him so that his big night was memorable for all the right reasons. I took him to the nail salon to make sure his nails looked good, ran him over to the barber so he would have a fresh haircut, helped him pick out his suit, and even put money in his pockets so that he could do what he wanted to do sans worry. I even had all of his friends come over to the house for appetizers and mocktails, and let him drive my car so that he could look fly pulling up to the valet at the banquet hall where they were partying. And I secured a table for him and his buddies at Justin's here in Atlanta, and paid a little extra to have the manager go over and tell Bryson that Diddy wanted him to know that he was pleased he was dining in his restaurant. Oh, Bryson went to the prom in style, honey, and every detail was handled, okay?

In other words, I make sure that I'm there for my sons during the times it really counts. Going to the prom was memorable for me—I remember it like it was yesterday. And though I had a nice time, to this day I wish my mom had understood how it, and other momentous occasions in my life, was incredibly important to me and she needed to *be there*.

As an adult, I can say that I understand why she may have done what she did, and I do understand that for some mothers it really is courageous and selfless to give your baby to someone who can care for him or her if you find yourself in a situation where you can't support your kids. I'm a product of this. My mother gave me to my aunt, and I had a great life because of her. My aunt gave me and my brother a *good* life.

At the same time, though, I'm still very bitter about my mother's actions. There's a part of me that's like, "Hell, I had a hard time raising my baby when I was young and single, too." I was only a few years older than she was when I had Bryson, but I was a single mom with no job and no money. Still, I made it work. And I especially made sure to hold on to my baby. When I held him in my arms, my love for him was so unconditional and full there was no way I was going to let someone else raise my child. If I couldn't do anything else, he was going to be with me. I simply cannot understand people who walk away from their children, just like that, without looking back. Eventually, my mother had a good life with her husband. You would have figured that at some point, she would have told this man, "Look, once we're on our feet and we're stable, I'm going to get my kids," or she would have said to me and Anthony, "I want you to be here, but your aunt and I think it's best you stay there in Georgia." How hard would it have been for her to just say that, instead of leaving me wondering, all these years, why she didn't love me the way a mother loves her child?

In fact, if I'm really being honest with myself, I have to admit, too, that I probably wouldn't be speaking to my mother if she were alive. I've never been to her grave after all these years. If I do go to my mother's grave site, I want it to be with the best of intentions. I know that people go back to the grave sites of the people they loved, and keep them clean and put fresh flowers on the sites and talk to them. A lot of times, they were very close to those who passed, and they missed them and found peace being there. But my conversation with my mother at her grave would not be so pretty. I'm sure that if I went, I would break down because I have so much bitterness and anger from her doing the things she did and not being a real mom to me. I wouldn't get answers to my questions if I went to her grave, either. It's not like she's going to come out of the ground and explain this mess. All that would be left is her silence and my anger.

I don't ever want my children to feel this way about me. The attention and praise I heap on my boys may seem excessive to some, but there's a method to my madness, for sure. It's a manifestation of my love for them. I don't want a day to pass by that they don't know that they are, above all things, loved.

Chapter 4

"WHO'S YOUR DADDY?"
SHOULD NEVER BE A QUESTION
A CHILD IS FORCED TO ANSWER

I learned on national television, in front of millions of viewers, that the man I called Daddy all my life was not my father.
That simple swab of my cheek, and one of his, and a piece of
paper declaring that the blood running in my veins didn't come
from him, changed our lives forever. How, after all, do I even
begin to reconcile that all I've ever known, all that anyone has
ever told me about my family, my blood, my history here on
this earth, is a lie? And how do you even begin to find out the

truth when the keeper of the secret—my mother—took her se-crets to the grave and left me to figure it all out on my own? It was such drama! You didn't see what was going on off camera. In fact, this has been an ongoing saga for years. There had been rumors running all through the family that another man was claiming me as his child, writing letters and making drunk phone calls to my people to say he might be my father. Mostly everyone just called him crazy and told him to get the hell on with all the "Nene is *my* child" talk. And my aunt who raised me told me for the longest time, just like she did on the show, to leave it alone: "Curtis," she insisted, "is your daddy, and that's all there is to it."

Still, I had a feeling in my gut that Curtis probably wasn't my father. Like I said in the previous chapter, I'd spent a lifetime feeling like my mother had me squirreled away in Geor-gia, like she was hiding me from everyone she knew—first from the life that she was forging as a single mom waiting for the fa-ther of her children to come home from the military, and later as the wife and mother to another family that I was purposefully left out of. But a few things that happened to me, as a child and as a grown woman, led me to thinking that the letter I'd read that fateful day—the one in which a complete stranger was try-ing to claim me as his own—was worth looking into. This stranger, I surmised, might be onto something. After all, it was only just a few years ago that I'd found out my *real* name. That's right: I'd spent more than thirty years answering to a name that wasn't the one listed on my birth certificate. And if my name wasn't even mine, then it made all the sense in the world that my daddy might not be mine, either.

WHAT'S MY NAME?

I was in my early thirties when I finally saw my birth certificate. My mother, you see, hid it from me all those years, held it close to her chest, even in death. To this day, I have no clue how she got me into elementary school or high school, how she got me my immunizations and doctor's checkups, how she finagled a Social Security number for me without ever showing anybody, much less me, proof that I was born and alive and her and Curtis's child. These days, you and your child can't step foot on school property, in a doctor's office, or across the border to Mexico without your kid's birth certificate, or they'll boot you with a quickness. But somehow my mother managed to get me where she needed me to be without that paper, and it never occurred to me to question it because it just wasn't something I ever thought about. As a teenager, I wondered where it was and what was on it, but I wasn't stressed about it enough to push. It wasn't until I got to college and got my first taste of independence—and all of the responsibilities that come with it—that I started a serious push for my birth certificate. After all, I couldn't go to classes at Morris Brown until I showed some proof of who I was.

"I need it, like, right now," I told my mother in a frantic phone call after a trip to the Morris Brown registration office, where the officials made clear that enrolling without a birth certificate was no longer an option.

My mother was quiet for a moment. I wasn't sure what she was going to say, but I knew from the awkward silence that whatever she was about to tell me wasn't going to be something I wanted to hear. "I'll get it for you and give it to you," she finally said, "but it may not have 'Johnson' on it. It might say 'Smith.' "

"Smith?" I asked, confused.

"Yeah. I can't really remember, but I think Curtis never signed the paperwork so they may have just put down Smith."

That was Shock #1.

I had been called Linnethia Monique Johnson all my life. My surname, Johnson, was the same as Curtis's, my dad. Why on earth wouldn't my birth certificate reflect that? Smith was my mother's maiden name. Was this some kind of hospital mistake? Was it her mistake? Did my daddy know about this? Of course, this was the question burning in my mind, but I didn't dare ask questions. A fight wasn't what I needed to have with my mom—I needed my birth certificate. Plus, on a much deeper level, I was afraid to ask the questions, because those questions would probably lead me to a truth I wasn't ready to hear. All I wanted was to register for college and start classes at Morris Brown.

My staying silent on the issue and keeping my questions to myself didn't win me any favors with my mother, though. As she'd done on many other occasions when I asked for my birth certificate, she simply didn't send it. Straight through until the day she died, she found excuse after excuse not to give it to me. Sometimes she said she misplaced it; sometimes she claimed she was sending it, and then "forgot" to follow through; other times she just asked me what the big deal was, why I wanted it so badly. This time was no different.

I asked my aunt about my last name, and she claimed

she didn't know what my birth certificate said, that she always thought my last name was Johnson because that's what my mother told her. My mother, she said, even stuck to that name when my aunt and uncle formally adopted Anthony and me back when we were in middle school. I remember this vividly, too, because when my aunt sat Anthony and me down to tell us that they were going to adopt us, we had a huge discussion about whether Anthony and I would take their last name—Thomas. My brother was quick to legally change his name to Thomas, but I refused. I wanted to remain a Johnson, because, really, it was the one and only connection I felt like I had with my dad, and I wasn't ready to give it up. I wasn't ready to let go of him and, by extension, my mom. My aunt wasn't insulted by this by any stretch. "Well, you're a girl," she said simply. "You'll grow up and get married and your name will change anyway."

I ended up registering for college without a birth certificate. Eventually, they stopped sending me letters saying I had to present one, and I started classes and nobody thought about it anymore—me included. I stopped questioning and continued on with my life with the name my family, my friends, my teachers, and everyone else knew me by for the entire eighteen years I'd spent on the earth: Linnethia Monique Johnson. It was just easier that way, easier to continue on as if nothing was wrong than to confront all of the inconsistencies and pain and secrets that would have come from snooping around and trying to find out the truth. Hey, I was eighteen, okay? And I come from a family where people like to let sleeping dogs lie. You just don't go around digging in the family past, making people talk about things they don't want to talk about, and exposing secrets that are secrets for a reason. Honestly, I don't think my family is any different from a lot of other families in that regard. Family members—especially the older ones—don't appreciate the fuss or the meddling, you know? Two of the most oft-repeated sayings for that sentiment, at least where I come from, are, "Don't go airing out the dirty laundry in public" and "Keep your family business out the street," and people in my family, and I'll bet in yours too, tend to take that seriously.

Indeed, I let almost two decades pass before I started asking questions again. This time, it was because I needed my birth certificate to get a passport. Every year, Gregg and I go away—just the two of us—to celebrate our anniversary. And this particular year we decided we'd go out of the country. Now, while I'd gone on plenty of beautiful vacations to fabulous places all around the United States, I'd never been out of the country before, and so I didn't have a passport. I couldn't get one without presenting my birth certificate, the birth certificate that I'd never so much as seen, much less had a copy of. And so I had work to do: I had to find my birth certificate.

I started by calling the Queens, New York, hospital I was born in, and they transferred me to the records department. The lady who answered the phone seemed nice—no-nonsense and surprisingly willing to hear me out. "I just need you to help me," I pleaded, anxious because I didn't want her hang up on my ass. I was from New York but had spent the majority of my life in Georgia, surrounded by folks who tended to believe the stereotype that New Yorkers are rude and evil and wouldn't lift so much as a fingernail to help somebody if there wasn't something in it for them. I didn't necessarily believe that, but I knew this woman had no real reason to help me figure out who the hell I was.

She listened intently to my plea and agreed to write down my information—let me spell my name, tell her my dad's name, my mom's maiden name, my birth date, and the address of the home I was living in before being sent to live in Georgia. Then she put me on hold while she took a look at her records. Within minutes, she was back on the phone, telling me she couldn't find any records of the birth of Linnethia Johnson on that date in that hospital to those parents.

"Well, my father's name may not be on it," I said quickly, hoping to keep her engaged long enough to want to look again. "And my last name might be Smith. Can you please check again? Please?"

"I'll call you back," she said simply.

I gave her my phone number, not expecting to hear back from her again. But sure enough, some two weeks or so later, that lady did call me back, and she delivered *Shock #2*: "Your name is Lenithia Bonita Smith," she said. "It took me a while to find this because I had the wrong information. But I'm sure it's the right one because it has your mother's name, Harriett Smith; the exact address you gave me; the same date; and the first name is the same, just with a different spelling. Where can I send you a copy of this birth certificate?"

You know I can talk and I don't have a problem saying what's on my mind, but truly, this was one of the rare occasions in my life where I really did not have any words. *Lenithia Bonita Smith?* The hell? I wanted—no, needed—to know what this mess right here was all about. There'd be no sweeping this one under the rug; somebody was going to have to break this down so it would forever be broke. First, though, I needed to have the paper in my hands, so I could see it for myself. "I really appreciate your time," I finally stammered before giving her my address.

ALL ABOUT MY DAD

There it was, right there in black ink, on the birth certificate the Queens General hospital in which I was born said belonged to me: My name really was Lenithia Bonita Smith. I kind of half knew the last name would be different; my mother had said as much. But why the spellings of my first name and my middle name were different was beyond me. I liked the name Monique. And here I was, really a Bonita. I can vaguely remember a few of my family members calling me Bonita, but it never really registered why. My extended family members had regularly jacked up the pronunciation of my first name, couldn't really wrap their tongues around it, which is why it was always easier for everybody to just call me Nene. And so when a few of them called me Bonita, I assumed they just couldn't wrap their mouths around the name Monique, either, and I can kinda see how people might confuse the two. So I never questioned why a few of them called me that over the years. When you're a child and a young adult, you assume your parents are telling you what's right, and if they say your name is Linnethia Monique Johnson, then dammit, that's what the hell it is.

But my mother clearly lied to me. Her signature was right there on the birth certificate—I recognized it. But my father, Curtis, hadn't signed the birth certificate. That meant that technically, at least according to the legal government records, he wasn't my dad. Which meant that my mother kept my own name from me all those years and died keeping the truth to herself. It also meant that the rumors about the man I'd called Daddy all my life may have had some merit. My mother took that secret to her grave, too. She had me registered at school, and everywhere else, for that matter, under some bogus-ass name that she knew full well wasn't mine, had me believing all those years that something so special, the name a mother gives to her child, was honest and true. What mother makes her child go through life not knowing her real damn name?

It didn't take me but two seconds to pick up the phone and call my aunt for clarification. I figured she had to know what was up with all of this, right? I mean, my mom was her sister, and she, of all people, should have been privy to the details about who, exactly, fathered her sister's child. They were close and didn't keep much from each other. But when I asked my aunt why my birth certificate was blank on the line where my father's name should have been listed, and why the spelling and middle and last names were different from what I'd been told all my life they were, she said, simply, "I thought it was Monique and Johnson." I knew from just the way she answered I wasn't going to get much more out of her. So I hung up and called the next best person: Curtis.

Now, you should know that Curtis and I have a history, a bad history. We've never been close; he's never been any kind of real father to me, no way. He wasn't even there when I was born, was off in the military while my mother struggled with raising a young son and giving birth to me all by herself in Queens, with no familial and little financial support from anybody. And even when he wasn't in the military, he wasn't paying me any kind of mind—didn't call much, didn't write letters, didn't send gifts, other than a card with some money in it on special occasions, like birthdays and Christmas. He lived in Seattle, and so it made it hard for him to have the in-person connection, I guess, but there was no love there. If there was, I sure didn't feel it. I missed having a daddy in my life, wanted him just to be there, you know? The only time he was "there" was when he'd find his way to Athens every few years; we'd get a day's worth of face time, and then he'd spend the night at my aunt's house, and the next day, he'd be gone again. All I know is that I wanted—needed—more from him. And I never got it.

But now I needed him more than ever. He was about the only somebody who could have known about this birth certificate situation, particularly the part about why his name wasn't on it.

"I didn't sign your birth certificate because she was supposed to give me the paperwork and she didn't," he said. Never once did he say in that awkward conversation that he didn't think he was really my daddy. But by the time I hung up with him, I started putting two and two together.

All kinds of memories flooded back to me, but one in particular stood out in my mind. One afternoon my mother took me out, just her and me. I was excited about and grateful for the one-on-one time with my mom—it was rare, for sure. She was living with her new husband and their kids. It was the summertime, Anthony and I were doing the standard summertime visiting routine—going up to New York. I can't remember exactly what we were doing that day, but I do know that when my mother said, "Nene, put on something nice and get your shoes and come with me," I was excited. She never took me anywhere, just the two of us, didn't seem to care all that much that I craved her attention and affection. My half sisters had her to themselves for the majority of the year; now she was actually calling me away from all my siblings and offering to take me somewhere, just her and me. Yeah, I stepped out of that house feeling really good. I put on one of my cutest outfits and checked my hair in the mirror a couple of times, and even put on a little lip gloss to feel special on my special time with my mom. Maybe she was going to take me to McDonald's, or to the mall to pick up some of the cute clothes she regularly bought for my sisters. Maybe we'd go to the park, I reasoned, or she'd take me for ice cream and then we'd sit and talk and she would ask me to tell her about myself and she'd tell me something about her and she'd say she loved me and maybe even invite me to stay with her for good.

But nope. She took me to . . . a gas station. When we got there, I sat in the car in silence, waiting. My mother scanned the parking lot, for whom I didn't know. Within moments, she beckoned a man—some stranger—over to the car. And when he peeked into the window, she said, "This is Nene."

He peered into the window and looked me dead in my face, but he didn't say much, just, "Hi, Nene." And then, just like that, he walked away from the car, my mother fast on his heels. They stood over by his car, talking and peering back at me and talking some more before my mother came back to the car, got in, and drove off without another word to me. Back to her house.

I was young, only about ten, but I was keenly aware of

what happened that day at that gas station in Queens. She was showing me off to this guy.

I never forgot that.

And I'll bet you my last dollar and a Louis Vuitton bag that the man she was showing me off to was my real father.

ARE YOU MY REAL DADDY?

You all heard the letter from the guy who claimed to be my daddy. I don't know if he is my real father for sure—we haven't taken any real steps to try to prove whether he's my father or not. Honestly, I'm not so sure I want to be bothered with another DNA test, with knowing for sure if we share the same genetic profile. All this DNA mess popped off when he called my aunt's house in a drunken rage. "You bitch," he sneered in the phone. "I'm Nene's daddy any goddamn way." That's how it started: He was calling around, telling people he was my damn dad.

And get this—he's Curtis's best friend.

Yup, that's right. The man who claims he's my biological father is the same guy who has been best friends with my not-so-for-real dad since the two of them went to high school in Athens years and years ago. My mother went to school with the two of them and was crazy about Curtis; back then, he and his brother, Mel, were quite handsome, I'm told, quite the ladies' men. In fact, to this day, they're both still pretty good-looking guys—they dress nice, work out, carry themselves well. My mother fell in love with Curtis and decided she wanted to make a life with him, and so she moved to New York to be close to the man she loved and got pregnant with my brother before she and Curtis settled in good together. Then Curtis was away on duty, and my mother was there, in a city with which she wasn't familiar, stuck with nobody but the one guy she knew from Athens—Curtis's best friend.

Uh-huh. Yup. Now here I come being birthed into this world smack dab in the middle of a really sticky situation.

Now, after that fool, Curtis's best friend, called my aunt's house and got all out of pocket with her on the phone, I called Curtis to find out exactly what he knew about the situation. He acknowledged that his best friend had told him on several occasions—most of them while he was in a drunken stupor—that he was my daddy.

"I didn't pay him any attention," Curtis told me. "I thought he was drunk and crazy." But Curtis also acknowledged that years ago, when his best friend was in the hospital on what he thought was his deathbed, he confessed to Curtis that he thought he was my real father. "I really didn't know where it was coming from," Curtis later told me.

And they're still best damn friends. Can you imagine?

Now, it was because of all of this drama that Curtis and I ended up taking that DNA test, and, it seems, the result came as no surprise to the man I thought was my father. You heard him on the show; he said he kinda figured I wasn't his all along. What you didn't hear was why. The problem, Curtis explained, was that my mother got pregnant with me while he was in the military, while he was gone. He did come to see her a few times in New York when he could get leave, he acknowledged, but he kind of did the math and the dates weren't adding up for him.

In the back of his mind, Curtis added, he had doubts. "She could have easily gotten pregnant by anybody," he told me.

When Curtis left, he said he told his best friend to take care of his girl while he was gone, but I'll bet you he didn't expect them to sleep together. Imagine what kind of mess she realized she was in when she got pregnant and she knew it wasn't by Curtis. As much as she claimed to love him, I'll bet she was pissed because she was in love with someone and went and fucked up and got pregnant by his friend. Just how in the hell do you explain that?

I guess this explains just why I've been the black sheep of the family all these years. She didn't want me because I was the constant reminder of her screwup, the constant reminder that she screwed up the life she could have had with a good-looking military guy with a good paycheck and the ability to make her life quite cozy.

It was her problem, and she was making *me* suffer because *she* screwed up.

And she held on to that secret until her death, and left me here to figure it out and clean up the mess.

That cleaning hasn't been easy. Earlier this year, I got the number of the man who claims to be my father from a mutual friend of ours who ran into him at a bar in Athens. I'm told he likes bars. And that he's a former fireman turned bum who doesn't have a pot to piss in or a window to throw it out of. Let's just say that I'm not a fan. I'd talked to him a couple times on the phone, but I didn't want to believe he was my biological father. The first time I met him, I was so nervous and scared—I couldn't hold back the tears. I had so many questions for him, beginning with how was he so sure I was his? And why did he keep it a secret all these years? And why didn't he come get me? How could he claim a child as his own but not be a daddy to that child—to me? All those questions pounded against my brain with every step I took toward him—I swear you could have seen my heart pounding through my dress. I was worried about what Curtis and my aunt and Gregg and the rest of my family would think about me reaching out to this man, even after so many of them told me to drop it, to just leave it alone. But something in me had to do it, had to take those steps toward him. I needed to take the first step toward closure.

This was the only way.

And when I saw him for the first time, I saw . . . me. And my son Brice. And a bit of Brentt, too. It was all in his cheekbones and those fat jowls and that bottom lip. In his eyes. The resemblances were undeniable. Funny thing is that, years ago, he said the same thing about me when he'd seen my picture at Curtis's house. I'm told he picked up the picture and asked my father who I was.

"That's Nene, my daughter," Curtis told him.

And this man studied the picture much in the same way I studied his face, looking for clues that would confirm me as his own. He concluded that I was, indeed, his child. But that's as far as he went with it. Until now.

I can't say that this man is my dad for sure. It's going to take a whole lot more than a handshake and a "we'll talk" for me to claim him. We'll see.

And I'm going to have to get through Gregg to do that, too. Gregg ain't hardly impressed with him. In fact, he's pissed I even met him. Whenever the subject comes up, Gregg and I get into some pretty heated discussions about it, that's for sure. I guess in Gregg's mind, he thinks I shouldn't be bothered chasing after a man who, after staying silent all these years, claims to be my father, especially since my mom isn't around to corroborate the story or stick up for herself or to call this man a damn liar if he's making this whole thing up. From a man's perspective, Gregg is also questioning what kind of man would sleep with his boy's woman—like, how foul of a friend/dude/human being do you have to be to sleep with your best friend's lady? As a father, Gregg also believes that I should continue to claim Curtis as my dad because, well, he's always been recognized as such. Besides, Gregg points out, a woman doesn't have to have a man's blood in her veins in order to be claimed by him—a point that I can definitely get behind. Gregg has proven this over and over again by being a fantastic father to Bryce, even though he's not his biological dad. And, of course, as a husband, my man is trying to protect me from a potential predator. Gregg always questions why, after all these years, my alleged real dad is suddenly popping up and claiming me. It's not lost on either of us that the man who claims to be my dad only insisted on going hard with the whole reaching-out thing after I started showing up on television screens. If you're already shady, and then you look up and see the girl you kinda, sorta think might be your daughter driving Range Rovers and living in a fabulous house and hanging with celebrities and starring in a television series, you might be inclined to reach out and see what you can get out of it. I am from a small town, and even I can admit that it wouldn't be all that hard for a hustler with just a little bit of game to come up with a fantastic story about blood ties in order to get his hands into my Gucci purse.

Honestly? I don't know what that man's motivations are for dragging up all these secrets after all these years. I just wanted my husband to support me in meeting the guy and see where I'm coming from on this. If the man I thought was my father all my life really isn't, and there is someone else out there claiming he is, doesn't it make sense to at least consider whether there's some truth to it? I know the circumstances behind our meeting isn't all neat and pretty and whatnot, but deep down, I kinda do feel like I need some answers—answers that can only be gotten by asking the questions.

I haven't had the opportunity to ask that man any questions, though. I've talked to him on the phone a few times since our first face-to-face, and, well, our conversations haven't gone very far. I told him that I wanted to get to the bottom of what happened between him, my mom, and Curtis and to find out for sure why he thinks he's my father. To tell you the truth, it was like he was drunk, coming off being drunk, or just really cloudy. He was talking about all these kids he has, including a daughter in North Carolina that he'd "forgotten" to tell me about the first time we talked on the phone. He just sounded confused. You can bet that that conversation didn't get very far. And when he called back a few days later, he didn't want to talk about my mom and his alleged relationship; he was calling, he said, to tell me some story about how he had a girl come by his house to clean up his place and she took his "last little bit of money." I didn't say anything, just let him keep on talking. A few days after that, he called again to tell me that he lost his debit card. I didn't give him a chance to finish his story. I just hung up on him. I knew where he was about to go with it—he was about to ask me to loan him some money. I'm not stupid.

Curtis says the man borrowed money from him before, and the day I met the man, my uncle Mel says he slipped him a couple of dollars. For all I know, he could be looking for money to get his next drink.

Maybe down the road, when he can get himself together enough to talk to me, we can have the important conversation—one that doesn't have anything to do with cash. I would like to know for sure whether he's my dad. I would take him to lunch. And maybe he could meet Gregg and my kids and they could get to know him a little better—take this journey with me. My aunt says she wouldn't mind meeting him; she even asked if I took a picture of him when I met him face-to-face, because she wants to see for herself what he looks like. And then, of course, she said he could "go jump in the ocean." I guess in her mind, he has a lot of nerve popping up after all the hard work raising me was done. That's my aunt for you!

If we do end up meeting again, it'll have to be on my own terms, though—with my ground rules. He'd have to come sober—no drinking before or during our meeting. And he would have to come ready to be honest with me. And even though I insisted earlier in this process that I don't want to take any DNA test to prove this man is my father, maybe—just maybe—I might change my mind and actually do it. Just to know for sure. I'd be much more open to it if he could sit down and talk to me and tell me what happened between him and my mom. But if he couldn't care less, I couldn't care less.

Besides, the story doesn't end there. I'm told that there might be another man—a former musician my mother may have been messing with while Curtis was away—who could be my dad. I'm told that he has a daughter who is a famous R & B star. I've not reached out to him yet, and I'm not sure that I want to.

And Curtis and me? We haven't talked again since we both got the test results. I can't bring myself to call him—won't really, because I feel like he's the one who owes me the phone call. At least that. I admit that we were both wronged here—the illegitimate daughter who was forced to shoulder the brunt of a horrible secret, and the man who was tricked into believing a kid who wasn't his really was. But dammit, he's the daddy. And I'm hurting. The least he can do is reach out and try to help make sense of it all.

It was a very hard, painful thing to find out that my dad is not my dad.

Now, I'm just . . . numb.

THIS I KNOW FOR SURE

I have to tell you, I don't know the lesson here. I'm just learning about all of these things too and trying to make sense of it all. How, exactly, do I reconcile that for most of my years on this earth, I was lied to, unfairly cast aside, and ignored by the very grown-ups who were responsible for giving me life and raising me into adulthood? Everything I've ever known about myself—down to my doggone name—has been thrown into question. Upended. Confused. I honestly thought that DNA test was going to show once and for all that what my family had been whispering about me for so long was wrong. I wanted—needed—my mom to be telling me the truth about me, about who Nene is. It never occurred to me that my own mother would lie to me and then take the truth with her to her grave. I simply did not see that coming.

I do know that Curtis has never been involved in my life enough for me even to miss his ass, so finding out he's not my dad doesn't really change much in terms of that relationship. We don't talk, never have in any meaningful way. Sure, he sends my kids birthday and Christmas cards, and he did walk me down the aisle when I married Gregg, but outside of those things, we don't have much in terms of communication. We'd gone for years without speaking before we took the DNA test, and I don't see us speaking anytime soon, especially if I'm waiting for him to be the bigger person. Curtis is a lot of things, but none of them involves being the bigger person. And quite frankly, I'm tired of putting myself out there and trying to make the connections only to have them broken for no other reason than that it's easier for family to break those connections than to try to figure out a way to make the glue stick.

I also know that a great lesson for women to take away from this is when your man is out of state, you should not be sleeping with his best friend—I know you need to know that. I mean, you could sleep with anybody, but his best friend? And what kind of father—if Curtis's friend is, indeed, my father—keeps that secret for years and years, and effectively dismisses himself from the life of his own flesh and blood? Seems like he raised the question enough over the years (with everyone, mind you, but me) to justify reaching out directly to me and claiming what was his. I can't say I can muster up the love for this man when I know now that he was sitting somewhere, convinced I was his daughter, and missing out on all the important milestones of my life. Where was he when I graduated kindergarten? How about when I performed in those community plays and participated in the dance recitals? Why wasn't he there when I was getting myself ready for the prom? How come he never bothered to reach out to his alleged grandchildren, or introduce himself to the man I love? Maybe show up to my wedding and walk me down the aisle.

In his silence, he missed life.

But you know what? The beauty of this big-ass bucket of mess is that I learned, albeit the hard way, how to appreciate the goodness in people who do right by me and my family, to see the beauty in the man who's been here for me through the good, the bad, and the ugly. Gregg stepped in and showed me what a real daddy is, by raising a son who doesn't share his blood as if he's his own, and stepping up and, with every ounce of his being, taking care of and loving the child he created with me. Gregg is a helluva father. He was there to help me put Brice in the first grade, and proved over and over again that he loved me and our union enough not only to create life with me, but also to nurture it, love it, and help it to grow. Gregg loves my boys like nothing I've ever known. Those boys are his—he advises them, works with them and for them, takes care of them, feeds them, and gives them someone to depend on. And he loves them deeply.

The way a parent—a father—is supposed to love his children.

And in my mind, there is nothing more true than putting your faith in a real man.

A real daddy.

I can't say I'm ready to make the mistake of putting my faith in someone who calls himself my "parent," particularly now that I know how to be a real parent, and have standing beside me every day a man who knows how to do it right.

Chapter 5

THE GUN SHOULD HAVE BEEN
THE FIRST SIGN

I met him at Sensations, a club in Decatur, a suburb of Atlanta. It was a Saturday, and I was looking good that night—not just because I was dressed cute, but also because I was happy to be out of Athens and chilling in the city. I mean, there wasn't anything cracking in the country; the movers and the shakers were down the highway, and on this night, my girls and I were a part of the excitement. The music was hittin', the drinks were flowing, and the club was packed with cute guys. What more could I ask for?

And then he walked up and asked those three fateful words that would change my life forever: "Want to dance?"

I took one look at him and thought, "Oh, um, nope, uh-uh," because dude was sweating like he'd just run a marathon. Ugh—I didn't like that. At. All. Who wanted a guy with a sopping-wet shirt and beads all up and down his forehead bumping and grinding against her? Not me, that was for sure. That was my initial reaction. Still, I gave him a once-over and assessed the situation. "He *is* cute," I reasoned to myself. And big and burly, just like I like them. And something about his voice turned me on a little; it was deep and booming. Strong. I liked that. Enough, I guess, to get over the sweating thing—so long as he didn't push up on me.

"Sure." I shrugged. "I'll dance with you."

He took me by the hand and gently led me out onto the dance floor, and as the music blasted out of the speakers and bounced all around the walls and the club got hyped from the energy and the flashing lights, our bodies moved in sync to the rhythm and then to each other and, soon enough, we were one out there, laughing and gyrating and laughing some more. I loved the attention he paid to me, the way he looked at me with those big doe eyes. He was respectful, but he made me feel sexy, like I was the baddest chick in the room. And I loved every second of the attention, so much so that I danced with him—and only him—for the rest of the night. He was a fantastic dancer, had command over his six-foot-three frame like you wouldn't believe. We cut a fine image out there on that dance floor, the two of us. And when we weren't dancing, he was buying me drinks while we chatted each other up at the bar; we even posed together for the club photographer walking around taking $5 photos of everyone. I still remember that picture—it was a Polaroid in a plain white frame. We looked happy.

I took that picture home with me that night, and, of course, his phone number. I used that number, too. Talked to him quite a few times about what young people talk about—music, cars, family, friends, how we grew up, our love for dancing and hanging out.

And within a few weeks, I was headed down I-20 with my girlfriend, racing to see this man who'd made me laugh and think of him even when I was supposed to be focused on something altogether different. My girlfriend, who was driving to Atlanta to see a guy she'd been talking to, dropped me off in South West Atlanta—better known as The S.W.A.T.S to us here in The A—where he met up with me so that we could spend a few hours together, just kicking it. He had a real cute ride—a two-seat sports car, and it was fast. He drove all up and down The S.W.A.T.s—me riding shotgun, him pointing out his mama's house, his high school, the superpopular hood strip club, Nikki's, and all of his little hangout spots in his neighborhood.

And when we got hungry, he pulled up into the Kentucky Fried Chicken drive-thru, ordered up two three-pieces, and rode around some more. Like we owned the city. I know it sounds stupid now, to grown people, at least. I mean, he drove me around the hood and bought me chicken. This is *so* not impressive to a woman with grown folk sense. But I was twenty; it was fun to ride around in a sports car and play music and laugh and talk and just have fun, you know? I thought he was a riot—cool and handsome and on it, like Theo from *The Cosby Show*, except from a not-so-nice neighborhood. My connection wasn't immediate, our chemistry wasn't instantaneous. But by the end of that ride, and a few more phone calls after that, I knew I wanted him to be my boyfriend, the first serious boyfriend I'd ever had. I'd gone on dates with other guys before him, but not many; in fact, I didn't lose my virginity until I was nineteen and in college. But this guy? I knew I wanted to be his girl. For the first time, I was in love.

And he made clear that he wanted and loved me, too.

Not long after that, we made it official: He invited me to his mom's house for his birthday party get-together—a big step for us, considering the invitees were his family and closest friends. I was nervous but excited for a lot of reasons: I was going to meet everyone he cared about and who cared about him; he was going to introduce me to his mom; and, because the party was so late and I was traveling by myself, I was going to spend the night at his place. Let me make something really clear, though: I had no intention of having sex with this man. I'd made that crystal clear when we were planning our weekend together over the phone. The deal was that I'd get myself to South West Atlanta, party with him for his birthday, and then sleep with him without *sleeping* with him. With this, he was cool, and there was no pressure from him for anything other than what we'd agreed to. First, we went to his mom's house and met up with his brother, who was out in the driveway shining up his car. I remember thinking that they were country as hell—had gravel in the driveway instead of concrete and 1960s wood panel-ing on the walls of their superold house. His mother was in the kitchen cooking a real country meal, too, just like she did every night of the week. I'd never seen anything like it except in the woods of Georgia. It would be a Tuesday, and she'd have turnip greens, black-eyed peas, candied yams, cornbread, and pigs' feet, like it was Thanksgiving—all that heavy, fat-laden food the country folk eat because that's all they know and trust in the pot.

Anyway, let's just say his family didn't seem like the city folk I thought them to be. His brother had a nice ride, though, had these beautiful rims on it. He was a mechanic for a Chevrolet dealership over on Stewart Avenue, which is now Metropolitan Parkway. Nice guy, for sure. The mother was, nice enough, too, I guess, as were his friends and extended family, who came to his mother's house to wish him well. He was loved, that was clear, had guys slapping his back and women kissing his cheek and offering him drinks and filling him with laughter and joy. It was a fun time.

And when the night was finally over, we went back to his house, back to his room. I wasn't nervous or anything; I trusted that he would respect my wishes that we not sleep together. But I was disgusted. His room was a damn mess. He had clothes strewn everywhere, the bed wasn't made, dirty dishes and papers and other garbage littered his dressers and desk. It was, in a word, nasty, definitely not meant for company, that's for sure. But I was too tired to protest. My feet were hurting, I was a little buzzed, and I just wanted to lay my head down and get some sleep. He cleared off a spot on a chair and put my overnight bag on it, and smiled. "Go ahead, make yourself comfortable," he said. "You can change in the bathroom if you want, freshen up or whatever."

I tugged at the hem of my skirt, sat on the bed, and smiled. "Thanks," I said, watching him as he removed his watch and his necklace and ring and placed them on his nightstand.

I wasn't prepared for what he laid there next.

It was metal.

And shiny.

And hard.

Made a *thud* when he slapped it down on the small dark wood table.

I could hardly believe my eyes.

It was a gun.

He laid it on the nightstand just as cool as you please, like handling that gun was something he did just as often as he brushed his hair or changed his shirt. It was almost like he was showing off, like he was trying to impress me by laying it there, not more than a few feet from me. His shoulders were squared; his huge body looked freakishly larger, like that gun made him two feet taller, two feet wider, two hundred pounds heavier. Stronger than any other man on the planet. I imagined that he was saying to himself, "That's right, baby, I got you. Nobody messes with me—I don't take shit from anybody. Be impressed."

I wasn't impressed, though. I was scared shitless. The barrel was pointed at the wall, for sure, but it might as well have been pointed square between my eyes. I'd never been around a gun before and my aunt taught us never to play with or around them, and we didn't keep any in the house. And I especially had never been around someone who kept one on his body. Only cops did that—cops and the bad guys. And I knew that if either one of them pulled a gun out on you, you better do what they say do, or else be really sorry you didn't.

This is exactly what was running through my mind as I stared at his weapon lying there on that nightstand. I didn't know if he was going to rape me, if he was going to slap me, if he was going to order me to do something I didn't want to do. All kinds of crazy scenarios ran through my mind, all of them involving me doing something I didn't want to do. Growing up, my aunt would say, "If you ever get robbed, give him what he says so you don't get hurt," and in my mind, this moment was no different from that. My thoughts were, "Oh, you need to be really nice to him tonight and do what he says do. Do it and leave alive."

Luckily, he didn't pressure me to do anything. He showed me to the bathroom so that I could change my clothes and wash my face, and then made room for me on his bed and respected my wishes that we not have sex that night. For this, I was grateful, and I went to sleep reasonably satisfied that he wasn't going to harm me in any way.

For sure, though, the gun should have been the first sign that he wasn't right, that this guy was crazy. For him to lay it on the nightstand, I didn't get it then, but I get it now. It should have been my warning. Hindsight is 20/20, but instinct is that third eye that gives you a crystal-clear picture of things to come.

THE FIRST HIT

I don't remember what we were arguing about—it was something stupid, I'm sure. But it was serious enough to him that he cussed me out and hung up the phone on my ass. I was like, "The hell?" I'd never had a man tell me off like that before and then to hang up on me so I couldn't get my two cents in. Whoa.

Funny thing is, though, I didn't get mad and blow him off and decide I wasn't going to talk to him ever again. Nope—I liked him. I don't know if it was a matter of me being young, stupid, or young *and* stupid, but I took his passion as his way of expressing his feelings for me. I kept telling myself, "Oh, he's crazy about me! What guy is going to get that heated about dumb stuff if he doesn't care?"

And seeing as he was my new boyfriend and I wanted to make what we had work, I gave him a little bit of time to cool off, and then I called him back, apologized for whatever it was I'd done to him, and begged his forgiveness. As incentive, I invited him to a party I'd heard about that night, a set at a venue not too far from Morris Brown, where I was a student at the time. For sure, we kissed and made up over the phone, and he agreed to pick me up from my dorm room and be my date at the party.

It was jumping, too. Everybody was there, all my friends from campus and a few of my girls, too. He and I twisted and grinded on that dance floor like I was his and he was mine—like what had transpired on the phone earlier that day hadn't gone down. I wasn't thinking about his ugly words or the sound of the dial tone or how we'd come this close to breaking up. I was happy because I was there with him, getting my buzz on and having a good time with my man and my girls.

And then he started tripping over something so damn simple and stupid. I still get crazy just thinking about it. I mean, it was just a dance, a dumb dance. Some guy came up to me and asked me if I'd dance with him, and I said yes. What was the harm? It didn't mean anything to me to get on the dance floor with someone who was ready, willing, and inviting me along, even if he wasn't my man. That's how we did it in Athens—you liked the song and if someone asked you to dance to it, you did. And when the dance was over, you either kicked it with him or, if you didn't want to be bothered, you said "thank you" and he went on his way and you went on yours and it was over.

Well, let's just say that my boyfriend, who had been dancing with other women all night, didn't see it that way. When I got off the dance floor with the other guy, he was there, waiting for me. His jaw was clenched—I could see the fire in his eyes. He grabbed my arm and pushed his face real close to mine. "What the fuck was that?"

"What?" I asked, looking at my arm as he dug his strong fingers into my skin. "Let go, you're hurting me!"

"How you gonna be out there dancing and shit with some other guy?" he yelled. He slammed my body against the wall; my shoulder and head smashed against it with enough force to keep me sore for hours after. "All up in my face and shit?"

"But I didn't do—"

He didn't let me finish my sentence. Instead, his hands—strong, quick, forceful—did the talking. And in one fell swoop, he reached behind me and pulled my hair so hard, he snatched my ponytail weave loose. Instinctively, my hands reached toward the back of my head. My eyes were wide and full with horror, my jaw hung so low I'm sure you could see clear back to my tonsils. "What you think this is?" he seethed, towering over and looking down into my eyes. "Don't fuck with me, hear?"

The music was so loud and there were so many people there, I'm sure that only a few saw what went down. But I was so hurt and he was so forceful and loud and scary, I felt like the deejay had scratched the needle across the record and shut down the music and everybody in the humongous room was staring at me, watching as I tried to adjust my ponytail and get the hell out of there.

I ran as fast as my feet could carry me, my eyes blurred by tears.

Away from that room.

Away from the crowd.

Away from him.

He came after me, apologizing with every step. I demanded he take me home and refused to say another word to him as we race-walked to his car, but he wouldn't let up with the "Baby, I'm so sorry" and the "I don't know what came over me" and the "I'll never, ever hurt or disrespect you like that again" lines. By the time we got back, he'd done a good enough job convincing me that he really was sorry and wouldn't ever treat me like that again that I believed him, accepted his apology, and agreed to forget about it and move on.

That's how it usually went down during our tumultuous six-year relationship: He would get mad at me for some crazy irrational reason, we'd get to yelling at one another, and then next thing I knew, he'd call me "bitch," slap me, push me, choke me. His favorite was the choking; he choked me so hard sometimes I felt the life sapping right out of me. It was really physical. He didn't care who the hell was around when he did it—he didn't hide his abuse. He would slap me if he needed to slap me. I remember hanging out with him and his brother—we were in the driveway at his mother's house, and I had my girlfriend with me. I don't remember what was said; all I remember is he slapped the shit out of me. My girlfriend tried to come to my defense, told him to leave me alone and not ever do that again. But it didn't matter to him. And then later, he was crying and apologizing and promising he wouldn't hit me again. Just like always.

Of course, when you're dealing with someone who is an abuser, he flips it like that—says, "I love you, I won't hit you again," over and over. And he makes you believe it. I had this fool cry with me many a time—he would hit me and *he* would cry. We'd both be sitting there, tears streaming down our faces, snot running, the works. And he'd be saying, "I'll never do you like this again. I love you. I'm so sorry." Oh, I hated to see him cry!

But you know what? He should have hated to see me cry. I wasn't the only one he did this to; he jumped all over his women who came before me and the women who came after me, too, and didn't even get in trouble for it! He simply did not know how to control his anger. If we were having an argument, he *had* to win. I could never get the last word. It didn't matter what the disagreement was about—it could have been about the dirty dishes in the sink or the color of the sky—if he felt like he didn't have the upper hand and then I walked off? Oh, he was going to come get me. And if we were on the phone and he couldn't get the last word? He was calling me a bitch. I tried to avoid the arguments, which you should know by now wasn't easy—my mouth is big, I'm outspoken. But I had to keep telling myself, "Hold your tongue, Nene. Just be quiet and leave it alone, or else you'll be eating his fist."

But he had a flip side to him. He was a sweetheart. He opened and closed doors for me, put the napkin in my lap, paid for everything, told the waiter, "My lady needs to order first."

He was everything you'd expect from a man on a date. That's what gets abused women all mentally messed up; their men seem to have this great side to them. And after a while, you hold on to that side of them and let those parts carry you through the bad days, until the bad days outnumber the good ones. Or he hurts you so bad that you run.

Or die.

I WANTED IT TO WORK

It was life that made me stay. Just a few months into our relationship—the first time I slept with him—I got pregnant. I'd missed my period and got a really strange addiction to Popsicles. I took a pregnancy test, and sure enough, there were the two pink lines telling me what I suspected to be true: that he and I were going to be parents. He was happy about it, too, told me that he loved me and wanted to be a good father to our child and that everything was all good. For this, I was so very happy, because I didn't want to be like my mother, the single mom struggling to raise her child alone. And I definitely didn't want my child to feel what I'd felt growing up without the love and support of my father. That would have been devastating to me. So I guess in the end, all he had to do was say he would be there for me and this baby, and I was going to make a point of making it work—period. That's all I needed to hear.

I kept the news from my family, didn't tell anybody until I was almost four months along. I didn't want to have an abortion, and I knew that if I told them too soon, my aunt and everyone else would encourage me not to have the baby. All they'd ever preached to me was "Don't get pregnant" and "Stay in school," and here I was, breaking two of the cardinal rules. And I was still living in my aunt's house, so on top of that I was stuck—stuck, that is, until he rescued me and the baby and we lived our happily ever after. This is, at least, how I'd had it all worked out in my mind.

Well, that fantasy didn't last long. By the time I was about five months pregnant, he totally broke up with me. It happened in the typical way young guys do it when they get scared and consider the responsibility that comes with father-hood: He picked an argument, got mad, and broke up with me, and then, to pour salt into the wound, announced that the child we made together wasn't his. And just like that, he was gone. His mother even got in on it. When I called her house looking for him, she got really flip in the lip with me on the phone.

"You're not pregnant by him," she said matter-of-factly, barely letting me get, "Hello, can I speak to your son," out of my mouth.

"This is his baby," I insisted. "Can't be anybody else's but his. I'm not that kind of girl to be with more than one guy, and he's the one I was with."

"Uh-huh, honey. Like I said, that's not his baby."

"Let's take a DNA test, then," I countered.

"It won't do nothing but prove that baby is not his," she said.

"You know what? We can take a shit test, this is going to be *his* baby, I'm telling you that right now," I seethed.

Months after that, I found out that that fool had gotten some other girl pregnant *at the same time*. I'll never forget it. I called over to his mother's house to ask about his brother's baby, because his girlfriend was pregnant around the same time as me. His sister answered the phone, and blurted out that his brother had a little girl, and my child's father had a baby boy.

"I'm having a boy, but I'm still pregnant," I said, confused.

She straightened me out, though. She told me that he had a baby boy with his other girlfriend. I swear to you, I almost had to go to the fucking emergency room over that one. I was shocked! He'd never told me that he got some other woman knocked up, and I had no reason to suspect it. But sure enough, when I confronted him about it, he copped to it—said that baby was his.

Still, no amount of insistence could make him claim my baby. I ended up carrying my son without any more contact from him. My baby came into this world with no one but his mama to hold him and care for him and feed him and love him. Without his father's love. I couldn't let it stay this way, though. My child needed his daddy, and damn if I was going to let his father walk away from the life he'd created. So when my baby was six weeks old, I marched into a child support enforcement agency where I knew they did DNA tests, and I got the paperwork going to prove for certain and for sure that he was, indeed, my child's father. I'm not going to lie—part of it was about making sure he helped support him. But mostly I just wanted my son to get the love he deserved from the human being who helped create him.

Surprisingly, he did what he was supposed to do on his end: He took the test in Atlanta, and I had Bryson tested in Athens, and when the results showed what I knew to be true—that he was my child's father—he signed the birth certificate. Around that same time, I learned that the girl who had his other baby dropped off their son and left, just gave him the newborn child and said, "Here. Bye." I guess she didn't want him or his baby. She walked away, and my ex was stuck at home to raise their son. With the help of his mother, he raised the boy—right up until he was eighteen and able to live on his own.

In the months following the test, he was still giving me the silent treatment—going out of his way to avoid me and steering his family and friends clear of me and my child.

Until, that is, the night I saw him at Club 112, then the hottest club in Atlanta. At the time, it was the only club to stay open until 7 A.M. Oh, they'd have it jumping in there—the celebrities would be hanging out and everybody would be partying hard until the deejay turned the music off. Usually I didn't have babysitters to watch my baby, but every once in a while, I would convince my aunt to watch Brice, and my girlfriends and I would ride down to Atlanta and dance until the music stopped, then head over to the Waffle House for breakfast before we drove back to Athens. Anyway, one particular night my girlfriends and I were coming out of 112 when I saw his brother, Alvin, riding in a convertible BMW out in the club's parking lot. And guess who was sitting in the backseat? I tried to pay him no mind. I mean, I was hanging with my girls and we were chilling and doing what we do, and I didn't really want to talk to him anyway because he hadn't bothered to call to see about me or our child.

He had other plans.

"Hey," he called out to me across the parking lot. "Where my baby at?"

"Where your baby at?" I asked, reeling back. "*Your* baby, huh? Really?"

"Yeah," he said. "I want to see my baby."

And within ten minutes of that simple exchange, he was in my car on his way back to Athens with me. I led him into my room, where Bryson was knocked out in a crib tucked away there. It was the first time he'd laid eyes on his son. Bryson was five months old.

The next day, he picked up Bryson and me and drove us back to Atlanta. I'd left Athens for good, to be with him. Despite his initially turning his back on me and our child, despite the beatings, despite the verbal abuse, despite the whirlwind romance and our relationship's subsequent monumental crash, I took him back.

Into my arms.

Into my bed.

Into my head.

And before long, he was beating me again. Sometimes he did it in front of his mother, whose house I stayed in on occasion while I was looking for a home for my son and me. His mother tried to step in a few times, but really, she couldn't stop him and, after a while, didn't bother to.

Still, I took each one of those hits for the team. I wanted so desperately for my son to grow up with a daddy in his life that I felt like I had to make it work, even if it meant getting beat on. And besides, I'd convinced myself that I loved him and that he was worth it. Believe it or not, I even helped him raise the other woman's son—that's how much I wanted our relationship to work. When I was at their house, I would help take care of that boy like he was my own son—we practically raised that boy and my baby like they were twins. Hell, they almost were twins—the other boy was only about two months older than my Brice. I have pictures of them together, they were very close. We dressed them alike, they learned how to walk around the same time, we potty-trained them and weaned them off the bottle at the same time, they both got the chicken pox one right after the other, and they started school around the same time. The two boys were virtually inseparable, and I wanted a hand in his raising because I knew that it was the least I could do for this motherless child. It was only right. And I loved his father and wanted to make what we had work.

After a while, though, staying with him wasn't as much about being in love as it was about being too scared to leave. It seemed that the longer I was with him, and the more I did to keep him from jumping on me, the higher and harder he'd raise his hand. Everything I did seemed to be about trying to keep him calm so he wouldn't go off. We'd have sex and I'd be grossed out when I felt him inside me—like I was being raped over and over again. Still, I justified sleeping with him by telling myself that I was doing what I had to do to keep him calm, to keep us together for the sake of our son.

That extended itself to being with him in public, too. If we went to a club, I'd have to hold his hand and get really loud and rude with guys who, not realizing that I was there with my man, made the mistake of asking me to dance or offering to buy me a drink. Oh, trust: He wasn't happy unless I was making those guys look like fools. "Can't you see I'm here with my man?" I'd say, making sure there was adequate enough bass in my voice to make it seem like I was mad as hell at the guy for even looking in my direction. He'd square his shoulders, like he was winning some kind of prize or something, just relishing the fact that I was making those men feel like jackasses.

Still, nothing seemed to satisfy him. He was a true Jekyll and Hyde, my first true love one minute, my nightmare the next. And finally I started seeing what a loser he was. He was nothing like me. I had goals, and he didn't have any, not one. I started dating him young, but I grew up, and it seemed like the more I matured, the more childish and stupid he became. I got an apartment; he moved in with his mom. I worked as a model trying to make something out of myself; he refused to work, and when he did get a job, it was something that paid hardly any money and involved little effort on his part. I simply couldn't do it with him anymore.

But I wasn't strong in my resolve to move on.

DO WHAT HE SAYS DO

I called the cops on him a couple of times and then refused to press charges because he always promised to do better and I didn't want him to get taken away from his son. We'd break up for a little while, and I'd try to date other men, and he'd drive by the condo I shared with my girlfriends and see the guy's car, or show up where the new guy and I were having dinner or a drink and he'd act a fool—cursing and telling the guy how I was his woman and he better get stepping. One time we got into an argument and he tore up my roommate Genesis's car because she used to let me drive it—busted out the driver's side window and left the two of us scrambling to find the money to get it fixed. He was certifiably crazy.

After a while, even my girlfriends got tired of him beating on me. They heard him call me all out my name, knew he was choking me and slapping me and threatening me. They were afraid for me and begged me to walk away. They'd sit me down and say, "Come on, say it with me, Nene: I'm not going to visit him, call him, or let him into the house." I'd say it, and even half mean it, knowing full well what would happen if I tried to play him off. I know it sounds crazy, but really, I'd convinced myself that it was easier to stay with him and take the slaps than to break up with him and suffer his wrath.

My final straw came the weekend Freaknik was popping in Atlanta. Freaknik was a huge party held here every year, in the beginning attended mostly by students from the Atlanta University Center. There was dancing and drinking, parties everywhere, a basketball tournament, a film festival, and, of course, celebrity concerts and things of that nature. Everybody would be here—students flying in from colleges and universities all around the East Coast, young cats who wanted to be around the college students and have a good time. They'd be talking about it on the radio and covering it on the TV. It was nuts.

So this one particular year, he and I had broken up, and I wasn't studying him, right? My aunt had Bryson, and I was hanging with my girls, and we'd decided to throw a little set at the condo. About twelve people were there, girls and guys we'd told could stay with us while they were in town to enjoy the festivities. We weren't doing anything, really, just sitting around drinking and enjoying music and good conversation, when he showed up at the door, banging on it like some deranged stalker. I was in the back changing my clothes when my roommate came and told me he was at the door, yelling and kicking and demanding he be let in. I yelled out to the guests in the living room to leave the door closed, to leave him standing out there.

Well, I don't know to this day who let his crazy ass in, but somebody opened the door, and in walks this fool with his pistol drawn. I started crying, begging him to put the gun away, to leave and let me be. I called him "baby" and said, "Please don't hurt me," and pleaded with him not to do anything to me.

He wasn't moved. "You better get in the car. Let's go!" he demanded, that gun pointed at me.

Genesis and my cousin, Eureka, could see the fear in my eyes. They knew what he was capable of and started freaking out—too scared to butt in and tell him to leave me alone but completely afraid of what that man was about to do with me. They knew he had taken it to the next level. The police had been called on him before, and he'd slapped me in front of a few people, too, but he'd never gone so far as to pull out a gun in front of a room full of people. He'd gone over the edge with that one. And nobody in that room dared stop him from taking me away. He told them to back the hell up, and they did.

Then they watched him take me out the door. And shove me in his car. And speed down the street, his gun still pointed at me.

He was driving erratically and bugging out, screaming and threatening me all the way to his house ten minutes away. He parked and jumped out of the car, and ran around to my side and dragged me out by my arm—the gun still on me. "Please don't shoot me!" I begged. "I'll do anything you want me to, baby, just please put the gun away!"

I knew that once I went through that door, I would be taking my last breath. He was going to kill me for sure.

He shoved me into the living room. The metal of the gun was dull and gray. His eyes were red. "You're going to have sex with me, right now!" he announced.

"Yeah, baby, I love you—I want you right now," I stammered, trying to sound anything but scared, like I meant every word. I knew that lying with him would calm him, knew from many times before this incident that if he was angry and irrational, sex would make him take it down a notch. It was a stupid mind thing I'd have to do. "I'm yours, you know," I said, kissing him on his neck and rubbing his chest. "I was wrong to leave you. I'm sorry, baby."

And with that, he dragged me into his bedroom.

Shortly after he finished, he forced me into his living room and had me sit on the couch. Almost as soon as my butt hit the cushions, there was a knock at the door. I could hear the static from the police radio, and it made my heart pump like it never had before. "Open up!" the cop demanded, banging on the door with such force that both he and I nearly jumped out of our skin.

He looked at me; the anger in his eyes was palpable. "I didn't call them," I insisted, raising my hands. Back then, we didn't have cell phones—just beepers—and so if we made a phone call, it happened from a house phone or a public pay phone. I was desperate to let him know that I didn't call the cops on him because Lord only knew what he'd do to me if he thought

I was responsible for bringing them to his home. Turns out Genesis and Eureka called the cops and sent them to his house. Thank God. "You were watching me the whole time, remember? I'm sitting right here!"

"If I open that door, Nene, they're going to lock me up," he said.

"No, baby. I'll tell them it was all a misunderstanding, I promise," I insisted—anything to get to the other side of that door.

He looked at me with those angry eyes, weighing his options and trying to figure out if he could trust me to open that door. "Okay," he finally said. "Do it. But you're going to tell them that everything is okay, right?"

"Yeah, baby—everything is real cool." I tried not to run to that door, to play it cool. But when I flung it open and my eyes connected with that officer's eyes, I couldn't stop the words from tumbling out of my mouth: "He took me at gunpoint!"

Almost immediately, the cops grabbed him up, read his ass his rights, and took him away. He stayed in lockup for almost two weeks before his mother got him released on bond. I had a restraining order against him, so by law he wasn't allowed to come within a certain distance of me. I wanted it—needed it—that way. Still, when it came time to testify against him, I refused to cooperate—I just couldn't do it. Crazy as it sounds, my heart went out to him. I couldn't imagine being the one who sent my child's father to prison.

And so he went free.

And I just went.

One night not too long after he got out of jail, I decided to loose myself from our abusive relationship—for the sake of

Bryce, who was five at the time, and for my own life, because I knew that if I stuck around any longer, he would probably kill me. That's real. And so I rented a U-Haul truck and left the condo I shared with Genesis while he was working his little job. I remember packing the boxes onto the truck and looking over my shoulder, scared to death that he might see us and figure out what was going on and get me. But we got out of there without a hitch, didn't leave any phone numbers or forwarding addresses, and I told everyone who knew me not to tell that fool where I was going.

Genesis, Bryson, and I just disappeared, literally, into the night, somewhere far away, where he couldn't find me again.

THIS I KNOW FOR SURE

People know me for being strong, loud, and unabashedly in your face. Nobody believed I was caught up in such an abusive relationship. Hell, I had a hard time believing it, but there I was, getting my ass kicked by a guy who claimed he loved me. A part of me thought that this kind of thing was normal between a man and a woman. I had, after all, been raised in a household where my aunt and uncle regularly cursed each other out. He never hit her, but they would go at it something fierce, and I grew up thinking that this was just something that men and women who love each other do. You get in an argument, you curse each other out, you go to your respective corners, and then the next day you're over it and moving on in your relationship again. Once I got out of my abusive relationship, though, and learned how to live on my own, found my independence as a woman and a mother, and started dating guys who wouldn't beat on me just because we didn't agree on something, I was like, "Damn, was I crazy?"

It took me some time to get to this place, though; it didn't happen overnight. While I was riding in that U-Haul with my stuff in the back, all I kept thinking was, "God, he's going to get me. I'm really in trouble if he finds me." He didn't have a number, an address, or any clue about where I was, but I knew that the minute he figured out that I booked up, he was going to hunt me down and kill me for sure.

And then I started wondering what he was doing and whom he was doing it with—missing him. Missing us. There were definitely some nights when I wished we could be together again, wished that we could live out the good times we had with one another. A few times, I even thought very seriously about calling him to see how he was doing, and to give him an update on all of the wonderful things that were going on with our son. That's how my mind worked when it wasn't occupied with other things. When my mind was free, I felt like I needed to call him. If I wasn't dating or talking to anybody on the phone, I needed to call him. I can honestly say I was addicted to him, like a damn drug addict in a crack house.

Thing is, I knew that his drug would kill me. And so I forced myself to write a note to myself listing all the things I didn't like about him, and then I taped it to my house phone so that every time I picked up the phone, I would remember why I shouldn't call his ass. I actually recommend this to the abused women I mentor, because I know that they, too, are unsure about their future and think that they can find more stability in an abusive relationship than they can forging a life on their own. But when it's written right there for you to see every time you try to reach out to your abuser, it makes it plain as day why you need to keep it moving. You read all the things you don't like about him, written in your own handwriting, in your own words, and then when you go to pick up the phone to tell him, "Come over here, I miss you," you can look at that list and re-member, really remember, what you *don't* miss and what you *don't* need and then get mad about it and hang up the damn phone.

My list was long.

1. HE SLAPPED ME.
2. HE CHOKED THE MESS OUT OF ME.
3. HE PULLED A GUN OUT ON ME.
4. HE KIDNAPPED ME.
5. HE'S A TERRIBLE FATHER.
6. HE CALLS ME NAMES AND YELLS.
7. HE'S IRRESPONSIBLE AND LIVES WITH HIS MOTHER.
8. HE GOT ANOTHER WOMAN PREGNANT THE SAME TIME AS ME.
9. HE ABUSES ME IN FRONT OF OTHER PEOPLE.
10. HE CUT UP ALL MY CLOTHES.
11. HE BUSTED UP MY FRIEND'S CAR BECAUSE HE WAS MAD AT ME.

And mind you, this was just a partial list. When I'd look at it, I would practically scream out loud, "I'm not calling that fool!" It got easier, too, when I started dating again. I was the kind of person who dated right away, which is really bad for somebody who was abused to do, I admit. You need time to heal—any mental health professional who helps abused women will tell you that the first day out of the gate. But for me, it was easier to keep myself occupied by dating. This was true especially when I started dating good guys, guys who were nice to me. Coming out of that relationship, I was always ready for the next guy to treat me badly. I'd told myself over and over again, "Okay, Nene, whoever you date next, be ready to fight him, because it's going to happen." But when they weren't fighting me, I started thinking, "Wow, what was wrong with me that I thought fighting was inevitable?"

But you know what? It was a good thing that I went through that abusive relationship because I gained so much strength from it. I wouldn't be who I am today had I not gone through it, I promise you. And from the moment I was on my own and dating again, I knew how to pick a man so that I wouldn't end up in the same situation with someone else, that's for sure. If a man yelled at me or called me a bitch, I'd never talk to him again; he'd get cut off immediately. I had nothing to say to him. I couldn't care if we went out a hundred times, we wouldn't go out one more. Keeping this attitude in dating was about self-preservation and certainly about protecting my child from any more harm. He never hit Bryson, but he hurt him by hurting his mother. No child should ever have to see his mother cry, and I wanted to make sure that my son would never, ever have to see that again.

This is what I say when I'm counseling women who've lived under similar circumstances. And there are plenty, honey, believe me. This isn't something that happens only to regular, average women, either. You wouldn't believe how many of the girlfriends and wives of these rich men—entertainers, sports figures, businessmen—get beat on. They'll be out at the gala in the most beautiful, expensive evening gowns and go home to their multimillion-dollar mansions, and those guys you all think are so handsome and so smart and so special are beating her ass all up and down the hallways of those big ol' houses. I've seen it—we all see it. Hell, one of my girlfriends got slapped in front of all of us one night while we were out partying together. We were all in beautiful evening gowns, looking absolutely stunning, and they got into a little tiff, and he just hauled off and smacked the shit out of her and then left her standing there.

Now, in my mind, her abuser was telling her, "Forget you—you can stay your ass out here on this concrete!" But to her, he was just being passionate, and being in a relationship with a well-to-do man she loved was worth an occasional slap or push or punch. "I love him so much," she insisted, "I can't see straight."

"You have a twisted heart," I said. "Your heart is just twisted. This is not what love is, trust me. He's handsome and has a lot going on for himself, but he beats your ass and that's not what love is about."

And right then, I decided to start my foundation, Twisted Hearts, named for my friend. See, I know I'll never make that mistake again, never allow a man to put his hands on me or call me names or play those mental games to have the upper hand in our relationship. I know what love is, and I know how it's supposed to feel. Your man is supposed to treat you with respect and dignity, and even if you have a knock-down, drag-out argument, he's never to call you out your name or raise his hand in anger, or abuse or mistreat you in any way. If he does any of these things, then he does *not* love you. Period. He is not worth your time and attention. Period. And you must get out of the relationship, not now, but *right* now. Period.

When I work with women through Twisted Hearts, I talk to them and ask them the same questions I asked myself when I finally got away from that crazy-ass man. I do my best to motivate them so that they know they're better than the situation they're in. What is it that you want to be? Did you forget that you wanted to be a doctor? A lawyer? You can still be all those things you dreamed to be—you're never too old. Think about your children: Do you want them to see you abused this way? Do you want them to grow up to be abused? Or abusers? If you don't love yourself, love your children enough to get yourself out of it. Do you go to church? Can you find God in you? Do you really think this man cares for you? Because you can't really care for someone if you punch her, beat her, slap her, and pull out a gun on her. Do you think he's the only man on the planet working and who can take you to a nice restaurant? Are you really impressed because he showed you a cute little apartment? Wouldn't you rather be single than tied up with this fool?

Look. At. Me. Let me be your inspiration. I was in all those situations—immature, young, and stupid, and easily impressed by things that didn't matter. And when I finally came to my senses, I promised myself never to let another man hurt me like that again. I made that vow. A big part of moving on was making sure that I'd never have another child unless I was married and sure that that man wanted the baby *and* me. I made good on that promise to myself, too. And now I have a happy life with a man who adores me, is a good father to my children, and wouldn't dream of hurting me.

Ever.

My ex is still in my life—always will be, because we have a son together. But the care of our son is where our relationship begins and ends. He wasn't really any kind of daddy to Brice, but I made a point of making sure I didn't put up any boundaries. If he wanted to talk to his son or see him, I wasn't going to stop him—my phone line and door were always open to him. By the time Brice was thirteen, he had his own cell phone, and so his father reached out to him on his line, taking me out of the picture when it came to their relationship. The only time I heard from him, really, was when he couldn't get Brice on his cell. He did, however, come to my wedding, and his other son was actually in the wedding party. I invited the two of them—the son because I love him like he's one of mine, and my ex because it was a part of my healing process. I did it because it helped me to put everything that happened behind us.

When my ex finally got wind of the show and saw a few episodes, he did call my cell to congratulate me. Whatever. I ain't studying him.

I've moved on—and I'm so much happier being me.

Chapter 6

"HUSTLER" IS *NOT* A GOOD JOB TITLE

Come on, now, don't front. Everybody has a neighborhood booster. You know the one: She'll come through the beauty salon or the barbershop or to your girl's house and maybe yours too with all the hot gear—dresses, blouses, pants, shoes, purses, hats, and more—and she'll lay it out all nice for you to check the tags and the material and the color and the sizes and what-not, and then she'll let you take it off her hands for a fraction of the price you'd get it for had you bought it in the store on your own.

For those of you who still don't know what a booster is,

let me make it plain for you: That's the neighborhood chick who steals goodies from the store and sells them to the folks who either can't or won't pay full price for the things they want.

Around my way, the neighborhood booster was Pam, a stylish little chick who knew what was hot and wasn't afraid to get it for you. Oh, we'd get downright giddy when we'd see her car pulling up because it meant that she was either on her way to get the fly gear, or she'd just gotten back from a run and was about to show us what we'd be wearing to the party on Friday. Everybody got the hookup from Pam.

Now, let me be very clear: I wasn't buying clothes from Pam because I was broke and couldn't afford the outfits I wanted to wear. I come from good stock, okay? My aunt would keep me in the latest fashions, would plop the Spiegel catalog down in front of me on the regular and let me pore through it for hours, folding back pages and circling with a pen all the cute little outfits I wanted for my own. And what I didn't find in the Spiegel catalog I mostly bought at the mall or at little boutiques like everyone else. Back then, Polo shirts were really popular, and I swear my aunt bought me one in every doggone color. Purple. Pink. Bright green. Dark green. Navy. Red. White. Every one of them. And the thing to do was to pop the collar—you know, flip them up and walk through the school halls with fresh, sparkling white sneakers and be cute, chile. I'd wear Gloria Vanderbilt jeans to the basketball games, or my Levi's, because they were the best fit for my tall, lanky body. And my friends and I would pair those outfits with our Members Only jackets, honey, and our collars would be flipped. You couldn't tell us we weren't something. And my aunt played a large hand in supporting my habit, too, that's for sure.

But I always wanted more, more, even, than what she generously gave. Maybe it was because I was taking my cues from my cousins. They were older than me and most definitely the type of girls who were somewhat bougie. When I hung out with them, they would teach me things—which guys were worthy of the digits, and which friends were good to keep around and which needed to get kicked to the curb, and certainly how to present myself in a way that made me look more mature and fashionable than other young teenagers my age. My half sisters were still in Queens with my mom, so my cousins acted like my surrogate sisters, the sisters I never had. We were together all the time, and what they had, I had, and what I had was theirs for the borrowing. I didn't have that many friends, but my cousins and I would switch clothes—I would get their stuff, they would rock mine. You knew never to loan out a nice shirt to a friend because that would cause problems; my aunt would be like, "Where's that shirt I bought you? I haven't seen you wearing it in a while," and if my girl had it and was taking her time giving it back, it would be a situation. Friendships would end over un-returned clothes, I'm telling you. But I didn't mind lending to my cousins, and my cousins lent to me, so much so that clothes literally bust out my superstuffed closet.

Closets were little back then. Today, a walk-in closet is a must-have, but back then we had one of those little closets with the sliding doors that would jump off the track, right? And that damn door would be leaning and all the way broke, running off the track, with my clothes hanging out of it. My aunt would be having a fit. But for me it was the cost of looking cute. Rarely did I leave the house without something on my body that was fairly new, and this made me feel good about me, just like it does most girls and women when they get to wear something nice and feel like they look good. In fact, I was so fly that in my senior year of high school I was voted best dressed, thank you very much. And, um, most talkative, which makes total sense considering how much I love to run my mouth. Dress and impress—that's what I did very well. So damn what Sheree says about the way I dress. I've been a fashionable person for quite some time.

My desire to look fly didn't go away when I went to college; it multiplied exponentially. My aunt bought my clothes while I was in college, and everybody else gave me an allowance so that I could buy my clothes, too. But when I left and I got into the relationship with my ex and I had a baby, I had a limited income, and considering my child's daddy wasn't kicking in any funds, I had to find a way to support my clothing, shoe, and handbag habit. After all, when I went out, I wanted to be the one walking in the room, looking and smelling like a star. If looking like money at the party meant I had to get my clothing, shoe, and purse game up, then that's what was going to happen.

That's where Pam came in.

If I went shopping at the mall and saw something cute but I didn't want to pay the full price, I'd call Pam and she would, well, handle that. Sometimes, she already had what I wanted in her booster bag, and sometimes, we'd give her a description and she'd cop it. Other times, she'd call us when she was on her way to the store and ask if we wanted anything specific, or if we had anything in mind. She was stylish herself so we didn't have to wonder about whether she'd come back with things we didn't like. Sometimes we'd just say, "Bring us back something cute," and a few hours later, she'd pull up in to the driveway and we'd run over to her window and take a look in her bag, or she'd bring her bags inside and lay out all of the cuteness on the bed. My cousins and I would pick what we wanted, and, more important, pay only half or less of what we would have paid for it at the store. And then, if after Pam left and I got my goodies into the house and I didn't like them or they didn't fit or the color wasn't right, I'd keep what I wanted and sell the rest to my people.

We called this hustling.

The police? They called it shoplifting.

And in my early twenties, I was rolling my fingers in ink and posing for the police cameras, convinced that I was going to jail forever.

Now, you know I always wanted to pose for the camera.

Just not these cameras.

LOCKED UP

See, what had happened was this: I was in town with my son Brice, living with my aunt and hanging with my friends, right? I'm sure it was a big weekend coming up; there was always a whole lot to do in Athens, what with the University of Georgia campus right there in the center of the city. There were always parties on that campus, usually thrown by the ladies of Alpha Kappa Alpha or Delta Sigma Theta or one of the frats, like Kappa Alpha Psi or Alpha Phi Omega. We would show up to those parties looking dead right, you understand? Or we'd go over to this place called DaVinci's on Baxter Street in Athens, especially on Friday nights, when they were serving chicken wings and garlic bread and Long Island Iced Tea. We'd get us the wings and a pitcher of the Long Island Iced Tea and sit and kick it. Either way, you knew that if there was a party somewhere in Athens with black people throwing it, it was going to be packed—and you better fall up in there looking good.

So on this particular weekend, I wanted to make sure I was supercute, so I called Pam to see what she had hanging around. Pam offered to pick a few things up, but she said she needed a ride to the shopping mall to make it do what it do. I obliged and invited a friend of mine along to keep me company while Pam worked the store.

We went out to one of those Premiere Outlet places out in the middle of nowhere and walked into all these cute little shops with Pam, pointing out goodies we were feeling. Once we finished rolling through the stores with her, we went back out to the car and Pam stayed inside and pulled clothes.

What none of us knew was that the mall was hip to what was going on. Security had been watching us the entire time—peeping me and my girl showing Pam what we liked, and later, following her every move through each one of the stores while she stole clothes. And they let her get all the way out of the mall, and into my car, and down the road before they sent the cops after our asses—sirens blaring and cops shouting through bull-horns like we were O. J. Simpson and Al Cowlings in the white truck, making our way from the murder scene.

It. Was. Insane.

Now, we didn't realize until they pulled us out of the car that we were being stopped because Pam had boosted the clothes. Maybe I was driving a little too fast on that country road or maybe my light was out—we just didn't know. We were thinking, "She's cool. Pam went in there slick, ain't nobody see her. We got our cute shit." We weren't thinking that they'd seen her steal all of that stuff.

While I pushed the breaks and pulled over to the side of the road, Pam was trying to get all the clothes into a trash bag so that it would look like she was donating goods to the Salvation Army or something. But the cops knew what was up: When they rolled up on the car, the cops knew exactly what to look for.

And they took all our asses to jail.

Now, I hated to sell Pam down the river, but girlfriend was the one who actually stole all of that stuff. It wasn't like my girl and I were in there stuffing dresses and blouses and skirts and things down into our personal clothes. So as far as we were concerned, there wasn't any way they could charge us with anything. Still, since all the stolen goods were in my car, and they had us all on film walking through the store, they figured they had our black asses nailed.

What's worse is that all of this went down on a Friday evening, long after the judge in the little hick town where we were caught had gone home. *Until Monday.* And the cops were insisting that the three of us be processed and stay in the jail over the weekend, until the judge came into work the next week!

My God, I can honestly tell you that I had never been more scared in my life. They fingerprinted us and took our mug shots, and then threw the three of us in a holding cell for a little while while they sorted out what to do with us. It was bananas! I tell you, that phone call to my aunt was the hardest phone call I'd ever made—harder even than the one when I told her I had gotten pregnant before I was married. My finger literally shook with every touch of the numbers on the phone's keys; I knew she was going to go off on me. Worse, I knew she was going to be sorely disappointed. And above all, I was worried for my son, trying to figure out how I would care for him from behind bars.

The conversation was not pretty.

She was pissed.

"Why would you be out there doing things like that?" my aunt demanded. "I can't believe you! Now I got to keep Brice for the weekend and put my damn house up to get you out. What if I lose this house, Nene?"

"I'm so sorry, Aunt Nellie," I kept saying. But I knew my words were hollow in her ears. I'd messed up big-time, and it would take quite some time for her to get over this one.

It was just terrible.

After the call, they threw each of us into separate cells. I was in mine alone, with nothing but a twin-sized bed, a mattress that was so thin you could fold it, a single sheet, a sink, and a toilet. I'm a little claustrophobic, so being in there literally stole my breath. The room was no bigger than my closet, and it felt like those walls were closing in on me at least an inch a minute. They fed us in those cells and we had to use the bathroom in there, too. You have to keep in mind that this was a little town and an even tinier jail and so there wasn't a whole lot going on there, or a whole lot of people in and out of the place, so I assume there wasn't anyone there to keep taking us in and out and giving us a whole lot of free time outside of the cells, so I had a lot of time to sit there and really take in what I did.

I couldn't get my son off my mind—I was worried sick. All I could think about was who would take care of him, make sure he was fed and had the right clothes on, who would make sure he was warm enough and that he got his special playtime. I wanted so badly to feel him in my arms, to nuzzle my face against his, to smell his baby breath, and to whisper in his ear that his mommy was there. With him.

But I couldn't. Because I was stuck in that teeny, tiny cell, left to consider the consequences of my actions over two of the longest days of my life.

Monday couldn't get there fast enough. They pulled us all out of those cells and drove us over to their little courthouse and stood us up in front of the judge. They charged each of us and then released us on bond; my aunt did have to put up her house to get me out.

I didn't want to rat out Pam, and I didn't. But I had to save my own ass, so I copped to nothing. I kept saying over and over again that I was just in the store window-shopping, but that I didn't take anything that didn't belong to me or that I hadn't purchased. And since they didn't have me on camera taking anything, and no one in the stores could testify that they'd seen me steal, the charges were eventually dropped.

THIS I KNOW FOR SURE

Please know that I am terribly embarrassed by all of this—I really am. I went back and forth with whether I should put this chapter of my life into this book, and all the way up until the final days before it was due, I'd told myself over and over again that I couldn't expose this part of me for the world to see. I've done a lot of things in my lifetime that others would think I should be ashamed of, but truly, this is the only thing I've ever done that I wish I could take back, that makes me hang my head in shame. What Pam did was wrong, and my encouraging her to do it wasn't much better—I know this now. I was thinking singularly about very simplistic things—looking cute and having fly gear—without considering the consequences of my actions.

By buying the merchandise from Pam, the stores she stole those clothes and shoes and purses from were hurt by my actions.

My aunt could have lost her house behind what I'd done.

I could have sat in that jail for God knows how long, and those police back there in those woods could have done me any old kind of way, and I wouldn't have been able to fight it one bit because my freedom and my rights were suspended for those two days while I sat in that jail cell.

And, above all else, I could have lost my son.

At best, I could have been locked away for a length of time and my aunt would have been left to raise my kid. At worst, child services could have decided I was an unfit mother and taken Brice away from me. The very thought of this *still* shakes me to the core, and this happened years and years ago, when I was in my early twenties. How, I kept questioning myself, could I have put him in such danger? How could I have been so very callous with my future and, by extension, his? The idea of his being left to fend for himself—much like I was left to fend for myself—was eating me up like cancer. It was ridiculous.

And I promised myself the moment those handcuffs were taken off my hands and that judge told me to get on that I would never, ever do something so stupid again. Everything I was going to do from that day forward was going to be about making sure my child was protected, raised with great love and attention, and, most important, that no matter what, I would never again put myself into a position that could lead to me losing my baby. I was the only one who would give him the love and care a mother could give, and if that meant I needed to dress in gunnysack because I couldn't afford the outfits I wanted, then I'd be the flyest gunnysack-wearing mom in Atlanta.

I hope and pray that when my children get wind of this they'll understand that I made a big mistake, that I've repented for it, and that I never again embarrassed myself and my family by doing something so foolish. My hope is that they and any other young people reading this book remember my mistake the next time they're faced with a hard decision that could land them in trouble—that they remember they have a choice in the matter.

And that they choose to do the right thing.

Chapter 7

WHAT YOU WON'T DO, YOU'LL DO FOR LOVE

*Y*es, I was a stripper, a woman who took her clothes off and danced for dollars. Let the judgment ensue. I mean, it's easy enough to do, right? Everybody assigns the same stereotypes to strippers: They're nasty. Gullible. Broken. Drug addicts. Low-self-esteem-having whores. In some cases, all of these characterizations may fit the bill. But that's not my story.

Simply put: My son was in private school, his father wasn't chipping in for pull-ups or food, I had no job and no money coming in, the rent was past due, and the super told me and my roommate that our condo owner was about to put us out.

So I did what I had to do.

I stripped because my son needed to eat. I stripped because he needed a place to lay his head. And I stripped because I wanted him to go to his fancy private school, the one that was going to keep him from becoming someone I didn't want him to be: poor, uneducated, and stuck.

It was about survival.

And survival was right there in the *Atlanta Journal-Constitution*, on the Help Wanted pages. There were a bunch of ads for "nude models," just the invitation and the phone numbers. Now, my roommate Genesis, the one who saved my life when she called the cops on my crazy, gun-toting ex, and I were models at the time. We'd met during callbacks for the Sepia Fashion Review in Chicago when we both were just getting into the modeling scene. We hit it off while we were waiting to be evaluated and weighed in at the first tryout, so we exchanged phone numbers that first time and then met again at a second tryout. When we both got chosen to be models in the fashion troupe, we signed up as roommates while we were out on the road and became such good friends that we agreed to room together even when we weren't touring together with the Sepia Fashion Review. The fashion troupes paid Genesis and me about $500 a week to travel with them all around the country. It was great money, big-time cash for us twenty-somethings. All we had to do was put on pretty clothes and sexy shoes and float down the runway looking fly, and then pack up our things, make it to the next city, do it all again, and collect our checks.

The problem was that the shows didn't last year-round.

The Sepia Fashion Review toured for only a few months, and if we weren't walking the catwalk, we weren't getting paid. In between gigs, we would pick up little jobs here and there with a temp agency, and Genesis had a job at Foot Locker, so we had a few decent money sources when we weren't collecting those modeling checks. Genesis and I shared a nice town house over in Hapeville, and the rent didn't seem unreasonable, especially considering we were splitting it. And though taking care of my son was expensive, I didn't have to worry about school tuition or paying babysitters or anything because he was still young, and occasionally my aunt would help take care of him when I needed to work. But we were young, and some weeks—okay, most weeks—we found plenty of other things to spend our money on, like food and cute clothes for ourselves—you know, the things we really needed and some, even, of what we wanted. The last thing we were thinking about, really, was saving a little something for a rainy day or keeping up our end of the bargain we struck when we signed that lease. We didn't have any business renting that condo; our sporadic fashion show checks, coupled with our penchant for cute things, usually added up to us skipping the "rent due" notices. We got away with that for a few months, thanks to the super. He was a black guy who worked for the condo owners, and all we had to do was flash a pretty smile and promise to pay in a few weeks and he'd keep it moving, let us hand in the check late.

But one particular time after we'd ducked the rent for a few months, the super wasn't hearing our excuses. The owners wanted their money. "You-all are going to get put out," he said, unmoved by our sweet talk and wide grins. "You have to pay the rent!"

I tell you, he didn't hit the door good before Genesis and I buried our heads in the Want Ads. I couldn't get put out. I didn't want to move back to Athens, and I needed to stay as far away as humanly possible from Brice's dad. I absolutely could not bear the thought of being on the receiving end of his back-handed slaps and his powerful closed-fist blows, and I certainly didn't want to stare down the barrel of his gun ever again. I needed to maintain my independence, by any means necessary. Getting put out was not an option. I needed to find a job quick.

Genesis and I had barely gotten through the first few pages before we saw it: "Nude Models Wanted." We looked at each other. We didn't really know what they were looking for— maybe someone to pose for an art class? Or pictures? We just didn't know. So, with Genesis listening in, I dialed the number and waited anxiously for someone to pick up the phone and explain just what we had to do to earn a check.

Turns out it was the phone number to the hottest strip club in Atlanta. I'd heard of it; it had a reputation as the most glamorous upscale gentlemen's club in Georgia—the place where all the celebrities, top businessmen, and ballers went to smoke the finest cigars, drink top-shelf liquor, and drop serious cash on the best exotic dancers in the business. The man who answered the phone told us what time would be best to come in for a tryout and who to ask for when we got there. Genesis and I didn't waste any time getting over there to check it out.

We didn't really have to try out for the gig. You don't walk into a strip club and get escorted to the stage to slow wind and grind so that the management can see you dance. None of them care about your moves. They care about what's up under those clothes. Ironically, it was a woman who decided whether you had what it took to be invited onto that stage.

She was known as the "house mom," the woman who takes care of all the dancers' needs while they're working. If you need a tampon, she's got you. You need a condom, she's got those, too. Need a new costume? A breath mint? See the house mom, and then tip her at the end of the night. She was kind of like the woman who sits in the bathroom at the club, handing out towels, lotion, and feminine products for change. Except the house mom at this club got bigger tips and had much more power. She was the one you had to get naked for, and she was very particular about her girls: No cellulite. No stretch marks. No fat. Only tight, perfect, sexy bodies were allowed in this club.

When it was my turn to go before the house mom, I was relatively calm. I'm not quite sure why; you would think that getting naked in front of a stranger would be a surreal experience. Nerve-racking. Scary. But honestly, it wasn't a thing to me. Slipping out of my clothes in front of her was as natural as taking off my clothes to get into the shower. There was nothing sexual about it, nothing to feel ashamed about. I simply disrobed, turned around for her to see my entire body, then put my clothes back on.

When Genesis and I finished showing the house mom what we were working with, she sent a note up to the manager: I was in. Genesis decided she didn't want to dance. "I want you to start today," the manager said to me.

I didn't know what to do or say. I didn't expect to get hired on the spot. I thought I'd have a few days for them to think it over, and for me to reconsider, too. But there I was, standing in front of this guy in this incredible club—no costumes, no pumps, no garter, and no clue how to do what I was just hired to do. "But, um, I don't even have a costume," I answered back nervously.

"That's okay. Go see Sunshine," the manager said. "She'll take care of you."

WANT A DANCE?

Now here's what you need to know about Sunshine: She was one of only about twenty black girls in the stable of dozens of dancers who were mostly white, blond, flat bootied, and big boobied—just the way the mostly white, extremely wealthy clientele liked their dancers. And even among the black girls, Sunshine was pretty much the only one who looked like she would fit right in at one of the black clubs. You know the type: round hips, big ass, dark skin, thick lips. She wasn't the cutest girl in the world, but her body was tight, she was sexy as hell, and Sunshine had enough clients falling up in that establishment to keep her paid. For sure, Sunshine knew the game, and she did what she could to help get me settled.

"The manager, uh, said you could help me with the costume," I said shyly.

"Oh, girl, I got you, don't worry," she said, pulling a skimpy white number out of her gym bag. She handed it to me, I tried to fix my face so that she couldn't see my disgust. I mean, really? Was I supposed to wear her already-worn bra and thong? They were clean—that much I could tell. But still, it was the same as putting on somebody else's bra and panties. No matter how much Tide and hot water they've had running all over and through them, they've still been on somebody else's titties and ass.

While I was trying to figure out just how I was going to put her drawers on my behind, Sunshine schooled me: When you start your dance, wear a top, a bottom, some kind of little wrap, and a garter. You have to take off your top; you don't have to take off your bottom. A table dance is $10. There are "happy hour" specials where the dances drop down to $5. Once you've gotten $20 out of the client, you come out of your top. Get another $20, come out the thong. Stuff the money in your garter, and don't ever let your thong touch the stage. Say what you have to say to get your client excited because the more excited he gets, the more money *you* get. At the end of the night, tip the deejay so that the next time you're on the stage, he'll play the hot music to get everybody—you included—pumped. Tip the hostess because she's the one who'll lead the clients over to you. Tip the house mom because she's going to take good care of you. And make sure the house gets its cut because the house wants its money, period.

"Look," she said. "All of this right here? It's just a means to an end. You get up there, you dance, you talk to your clients, you have a few drinks, and before you know it, you done pulled in that money. Don't even trip about it," she said, just as easy.

Like it really was easy.

My first dance was anything *but* easy. I was a nervous wreck—my legs were a wiry mess walking through the aisle and across the smaller stage, where a piano sat, waiting for me to climb atop and reveal Sunshine's costume, which I'd hurriedly climbed into. I'd always thought I was sexy, was never ashamed of my body or worried about how I looked in the nude. But I have to admit that with every step toward that piano, my heart beat faster and my breath got heavier. I felt like every eye in the place was on me, that each and every man in the house was deciding in his mind at that very moment whether I was hot enough, pretty enough—sexy enough. I was, simply put, overwhelmed.

But somehow, my legs carried me up there anyway.

And the music pumped through the speakers.

And I looked over nervously at the other girls, the ones popping their booties for the clients on the floor, the girl up on the main stage twirling around the pole like she was a slippery snake, the ones sitting at the bar sipping their drinks and bouncing their asses on the chairs to entice potential clients.

And then the house announcer called out my stage name—Silk.

I started to move.

Because it was my job to move.

And I had to move if I wanted to feed my son and keep a roof over our heads.

I'll tell you this much, I didn't know what the hell I was doing that first time. But I learned quick, fast, and in a hurry, that's for sure. I'm a woman, see? And there are just some things I think are innate to us, some instances where, as a woman, your natural instincts kick in. Think about it: The first time a woman has a baby, she has no idea how to hold that child the right way, or how to put that baby's mouth over her breast to nurse him, or even how to change a diaper on a squirmy, tiny little newborn.

But there's something inside her that makes her instinctively know what to do.

It's the same thing with dancing, I guess. You're nervous and shy about it, but your natural instincts as a woman kick in and you automatically know what's sexy, what you think the guy would like to see you do. Nobody's giving you lessons at the club, telling you to "turn around like this" and "shake like that." You figure that shit out. I've always been a good dancer—always good at picking up routines—and so if I saw another girl doing a move and it was working for her, I did that, too. And after a while, the instincts kicked in. And the more I used them, the more money those men laid at my feet. I swayed and twisted my body slowly, rubbing myself in places I knew they'd die to touch, and then I tapped my garter as if it were an ATM machine, making it clear to the men I was turning on that if they wanted more, they better dig deeper into their pockets and pay me.

I was extremely uncomfortable. But I did it.

And once I got back upstairs to Sunshine and I counted my money? I was like, "Oh, this ain't half bad." I know that sounds crazy, but that's where my mind was then. Sunshine saw me grinning and knew I'd finally come around to seeing it like all the other dancers at the club saw it: This was quick, easy money. Plain and simple.

"Go back and try it again." Sunshine laughed.

I tried it again, and I came back with more money. And after a while, I wasn't uncomfortable or embarrassed anymore. In fact, I felt powerful in front of those men. They were obviously there to see what I had, and I quickly realized that those men weren't there to make me feel bad about myself. Quite the contrary, they were there to make me feel good. They weren't there to argue with me or question what I was wearing or pass judgment on me like women do to other women. They were there to tell me how beautiful I was, and how they'd had fights with their wives and I was giving them relief from marriage problems and the mess on their jobs—that I was their therapy. Mostly, they were there to drink beer and hang with their boys and see us pretty girls. And if they paid enough, we pretty girls might even touch them—their shoulders, their legs, their hands, their laps—turn them on and have them coming out their pockets for more. I had everything it takes to be one of the best strippers in the game—never-ending legs, succulent lips, alluring hips, and intoxicating breasts that stood at attention and practically begged to be squeezed. And there was a flood of men— single and married—who would stop in their tracks and spend down to their last dime to get an up-close look at my body. As I danced, I would bend over slightly toward them and whisper in their ears, "God, you turn me on" and "I can't wait for my body to touch yours, Daddy." They'd melt right there in front of me, and get rock-hard, too. Some of them ran to the men's room to "relieve" themselves so many times during my shift I thought they were going to hurt themselves. I fulfilled their dreams and their fantasies—and got paid good money to make them crazy.

By the end of that first night, I was walking out the door with $600 in cash in my purse, and all I had to do for it was show my titties for a couple of hours. I knew on the drive home that I was going to be dancing for a minute because the money was good. Real good. I looked at it the same way a drug dealer does being in the game—you keep doing it because it's quick and it's easy. You say to yourself, "I want to go to the club with my girlfriends and have a good time tonight. Let me go up in here for a couple of hours and make a quick $600, and then go have a nice time tonight." Or "I have to pay my car note and the rent is due, let me pull a double shift and bring home a few grand, and if I need a few more dollars, I come back, get another grand or two, and then go spend it." It sounds crazy, but it was so fast and easy to do, and I felt like I had the power because I was the woman all those men adored, honey. They loved them some Silk. And Silk didn't have to do anything she didn't want to do. I could go as far as I wanted to go and then stop and not have sex with him, and take all of his cash in the process. Please and tease, that was the name of the game. And my rule was to preserve my dignity at all times, to remember that I was there for a reason. To achieve a purpose. And never, ever to cross the line for any man, for any reason, for any amount of money. I was a saleswoman, but I sold dreams—not ass.

For the life of me, I couldn't figure out why women would go out on the street and prostitute themselves when they could just fix up cute, get up on the stage, and let men pay them just to look. Now don't get me wrong—there was some mess popping off in that club. Back in the VIP room, a gentleman could definitely find some happy endings. But that wasn't the job of every girl in the club. Most of us stuck to dancing, but if we took a man in the back room for a private dance and he got all hot and bothered and wanted more than a striptease, we knew to go get one of the girls who sell, introduce her to him, and let her take care of that while we went back out front to make our money dancing. I wouldn't let a guy put so much as a finger on me in the club. Many men had tried to sneak a feel, a rub, a touch, but my job was to keep their fantasy hot and not allow anyone to touch me. This would make a man crazy, and he would keep spending more and more money with the hope that he would be able to lay hands. If he tried that shit with me, though, security put his ass out on the curb.

It was the ultimate power trip.

NASTY GIRLS

Over time, having this control—this power over men—actually built up the self-esteem I'd lost during the five years I suffered indescribable abuse at the hands of my ex. What he took from me, others paid to enjoy. And with every piece of clothing I took off, the more I got my life back. I worked this body like a well-oiled machine, and every movement got me closer to my goal of financial independence for me and my child.

I learned pretty quickly, too, that I wasn't there to meet any men. I mean, there were good men to be had there; a few of the dancers had boyfriends—nice guys—who would stop by the club to see them and hang out for a while while their girl-friends danced. But it took me just one time to figure out that getting romantically interested in a customer wasn't for me. His name was Tony, and he was handsome, a lot of fun, had a big personality, and called himself trying to woo me. Now, I had rules for working in the club, and chief among them was that I'd never fraternize with the customers outside work. While the other girls kicked it with men they were attracted to, I was rush-ing out to pick up my child from school and get on home. But this one customer? I was really attracted to him. He was balling—he drove a Benz, and every time he came into the club, he spent a lot of money. He'd always get a dance with me and flirt with me and I'd flirt right on back—not in a dancer, "get that money" way but in a "you're cute and I'd like to get to know you better" way. We'd joke and laugh together, and he'd keep telling me how much he wanted to take me out on a date—a real date. Just me and him. And soon, I started telling myself that I might even consider going out with him—breaking my rule and giving him a chance. And one night, we exchanged numbers. Neither of us ever used them—I didn't call him, and he didn't call me. But that exchange of phone numbers put both of us on notice that we were feeling one another and willing to see where this thing would go.

Anyway, he came to the club one day and I could tell he was hot and bothered and wanted me to do more than just dance for him. "Let's go into the VIP room," he said.

Now here's what you need to know about the "VIP" room at the club I used to dance in: The men who went in there were going in there for a lot more than lap dances. If they went in there, it was to get blow jobs or to have sex with one of the dancers—we called it "turn a trick." Be clear: There were some really nice men who came to the club just to unwind and have a good time, and I wasn't about to make any judgments on the kind of men they were for patronizing strippers. But what I couldn't be bothered with was a man who wanted to turn a trick in the club. And here was Tony, all hot and bothered, wanting to know if I would go further with him.

I told him quickly that I wouldn't. But if he really wanted to go there, he should holler at this other stripper I knew who would do whatever he wanted her to do. That was her job, not mine. And that fool said, "Go get her." Within minutes, she and that fool were walking into the VIP room to make it do what it do.

I gave it a few minutes to see if this man, who had just told me not more than a few nights ago that he wanted to take me out on a real date because he liked me, was really going to go in the back room and have sex with another woman. I told myself that if he had any kind of class, he wouldn't do anything with her—that he would just say, "Oh, I wasn't serious—I didn't really want to do *that* with *her.*"

But, sure enough, when I went and peeked into the VIP room, what I saw just shocked the crap out of me.

There was Tony.

Having sex.

And looking me dead in the eye while he was doing it.

There were no words exchanged between us—the looks we gave each other said it all. I imagined that he was saying in his mind, "Well, she ain't never going to fuck me." My look said, "Uh-huh, I see you, you nasty ass."

It was just horrible! I don't even think he had on a condom. I mean, if you're going to turn a trick in the club, at least use a condom! They had plenty of them in the men's room— there was a guy in there whose sole job was to keep the bathroom clean and give the guys condoms if they needed them. I'm thinking that any man with sense who's gotta go home to his girlfriend or wife—or, hell, who wants to protect himself— would say, "Hmm, I'm about to turn this trick—I'm gonna need a condom." It takes only a second. But not Tony. It just blew my mind that he was willing to have unprotected sex with that woman, knowing full well that he wasn't the first guy she'd slept with that night, and probably wouldn't be the last. Ugh.

Later, I found out that he lived with a woman and had a child—can you believe it? He kept coming back to the club, too. But we never talked again, you can believe that. Not one word.

See? That's the huge misconception—that all women who work in the clubs are nothing more than tricks. Sure, there are some bottom bucket clubs full of some bottom bucket bitches. But let me tell you, the club where I worked was full of all kinds of ladies—some of them paying their way through nursing school, some of them students at Clark-Atlanta and Spelman, from good homes, going to class during the day and dancing at night. There were hood girls, cute girls, bougie girls—cliques worse than the ones you find in a high school lunchroom. Stand out in that parking lot, though, and those girls would be pulling out in BMWs and Benzes, driving to their apartments full of nice furniture, with the phone numbers of professional football and basketball players, lawyers, doctors, business owners. You can go over to Magic City tonight, and you'll see Benzes and Beamers and Range Rovers, and all of the dancers driving them will have their weaves fixed and their makeup done, and live like regular, everyday people.

I was that regular, everyday girl, too, you know. I worked the day shift and used the money I made to put my son in a private school I could afford now that I was bringing in good money. I'd drive him there in my Honda. He wore this cute little green uniform, and he'd beg me to take him to Hardee's every day. He cracked me up when we pulled into the drive-thru. He always got the butter biscuit with one side of grape jelly and I'd hand it to him and he'd tear that sucker up. He loved his mornings with me, and I loved them, too—because I could provide for him. He wanted for nothing. I quickly stacked paper for my and my son's future. My rent and all my bills were paid, my two new cars were paid in full, my son's tuition was paid a whole year in advance. We breathed easy every day.

After I dropped him off at school, I'd head to work and dance while he was learning his ABCs. It was easier for me this way because I didn't have anyone to watch my son. My family lived in Athens, and I didn't have any babysitters on stand-by waiting to watch my son and help him with his homework and feed him dinner and put him to sleep at night. So I worked the breakfast and lunch crowd. Guys would be at the breakfast buffet, filling up their plates with eggs and grits and biscuits and eating it all while they watched me dance. By around 5 P.M., I'd run over to the day care center and pick up my baby and be on my way to my ordinary life at my apartment, where my child had his own room, I had a new Honda Accord and a new Mustang parked out in the parking lot, and I could keep myself looking good from head to toe. I worked as an exotic dancer from the time Brice was three until about age six. He didn't know a thing about it because when I came home, I wasn't Silk. The moment I stepped out of that club and got into my car, I was Nene, Brice's mom. There wasn't a job on this earth that could give me all of this, as far as I was concerned. And if someone told me I had to leave the club, I would have died.

But I'll tell you what made me almost die a thousand deaths: the night two guys from Athens walked in and saw me giving a lap dance to a client. I don't know what they were doing in Atlanta, and it was just shitty luck that they wound up coming to the strip club during my shift, but there they were, smoking their cigars, drinking their beers, and watching me do my dance. I looked over at them and knew I was busted. Nobody in my family knew I was dancing. I wasn't embarrassed by how I made my living, but I didn't want to face my aunt. She would have been extremely disappointed in me, and I just couldn't face that—not with her.

I went on with my flow and then took a break and spoke to them for a few minutes about nothing—we kept it at "Hey, how you been? Good to see you"—and then I went back to work and they went back to their beers and we didn't have any more contact again. It took me only a few minutes to reason with myself that they wouldn't go back and say anything to anybody. "Hell," I told myself, "they were in the strip club, too, so . . ."

But a few weeks later, my aunt called and made clear that the two guys from my hometown sang like canaries. "I heard you working in them clubs," she said. My heart practically leaped out of my chest, that's how hard it was pumping.

"What are you talking about? I don't work in any clubs. Who told you that?" I asked, trying to use a tone that made it seem like I was disgusted. "I don't know who told you that lie."

I hated lying to her, but on the real? My aunt wasn't paying any bills, she wasn't babysitting my son, and I had absolutely no desire to move back to Athens to figure out some other kind of way to make money. I had to do what I had to do. Of course, I didn't want my family thinking less of me. But it was what it was.

By the time I finished my Oscar-worthy denials, my aunt hung up reasonably convinced that I wasn't a stripper. The very next day, though, I quit that club.

But I didn't stop stripping.

I just went underground.

THE JACK SHACK

When they're trying to be nice about it, people call them "lingerie shops"—places where a man can go into a private booth and have a lady dressed in sexy lingerie dance for him. But people in the business know them as "jack shacks," and the dancers are clear about their role: The ladies turn the guy on while he masturbates and keep working him for money until he ejaculates.

I really liked this gig.

Oh, the masturbating part I could have certainly done without. I couldn't stand to watch them pull out their dingalings and touch themselves, and the, um, "ending" was especially disgusting to me. For a long time, I couldn't dare see someone masturbate. I'd be like, "I'm outta here," because so many guys are willing to do that in the club, no matter who is watching or how nasty it is or what it looks like. Men do some really filthy things in the club. I can tell you this much: You can go to the strip club right now and a lot of women in there go with each other because they're totally turned off by the guys and the things they come in there and do. It's like, how can a guy be with a woman and claim to be capable of being faithful and then go in the club and turn tricks and all that mess with other girls? There are so many guys willing to do that in the club, trust me when I tell you. Of course, I would much rather a guy masturbate than have sex with a girl with no condom on; at least he's going the safe route. Still, if they were up in there for anything more than a lap dance, their behavior was all quite nasty to me.

But I liked working in the jack shack more, though, because I could make $500 off one guy, just by turning him on. When they'd come in, the front of the house would give them a "menu," and on it were prices for the different amounts of time they could spend with a dancer. A forty-five-minute session was $200. I'd keep 60 percent of that and give 40 percent to the house, and then take the gentleman into the room and make him keep giving me money until he got to where he needed to go. I'd be working him, too, talking all kinds of sweet talk and telling all kinds of lies. "How much do you want this? Don't you want me, Daddy? You're so damn sexy—I want you so bad. What you gonna do with it?" Of course, he'd be nodding and saying yes and telling his lies, too—talking all kinds of shit about what he was going to do and moaning like a damn baby. The only one who would be getting excited by all that talk was the man saying it to me; in the meantime, I'd be getting paid for getting him to touch his own body. Dumb asses.

The best thing about the jack shack was that I could maintain a reasonable amount of anonymity. I could see who was coming up in there before he got into the door, and if someone I knew didn't need to see me was approaching the door, I could go stand in the back while he picked from the menu, found a girl he liked, and headed into one of the rooms. There were maybe ten girls working in the whole place, in shifts of maybe five. The owners were pretty easygoing. If I couldn't work on Tuesday, it wasn't a big deal. And if I could find someone to watch my son, I could pull a double shift if I needed more cash. It all worked out.

After a while, though, when I felt like it was safe to return, I found my way back to the strip club. I worked the stage as a dancer in another upscale gentlemen's club, this one just as luxurious as the first, with a cigar bar, a fancy restaurant menu, and only the best, tightest, most beautiful dancers in the business. I danced only a little while, though. I had my eyes on a much bigger prize than the dollars I made doing stripteases.

I'd met a man.

He was good to me.

And good for me.

I knew that if what we had was meant to be, I'd have to come clean to him about what I did for a living, and if he was still interested in forging a long-lasting relationship with me, I'd eventually have to quit—prepare myself for his love and get ready to live a good, stable life with a man who was successful enough to provide the lifestyle I was accustomed to.

When I told Gregg that I was an exotic dancer, he didn't believe me, thought I was pulling his chain. "Come down to the club, then," I insisted. "I'll show you."

He came, all right.

And he didn't judge me.

He just showed me love.

And not more than a few days later, Gregg asked me to make a change, to hang up my seductive costumes and my sexy moves and let him talk to the manager about getting me a gig working as a hostess. He wanted me to change jobs, you see, because he was about to help change my life—to forge a life with me. I needed a change, see, because I wanted to be with this man who was willing to take care of me and my son and provide a good life for us, the kind of stability that Brice and I craved. Deserved. And I knew that that kind of life could not be had with me taking my clothes off for other men.

So Gregg talked to the manager. I wouldn't have had a problem asking for myself, but I didn't mind Gregg doing it, and anyway, he wanted to. The manager agreed to let me work as a hostess, seating the gentlemen as they came into the club, making sure they got their cigars and drinks quickly, and serving up girls who fit the description of dancers the clients wanted at their tables, counting out the drawer at the end of the night, and helping to close the club down. It was by no means as lucrative as working up onstage. I got a regular paycheck every week, for $500 only, plus tips from all the dancers. But it was enough for me to start a new life.

THIS I KNOW FOR SURE

The question was a shock, like someone had thrown a gallon of ice water in my face. The fans are always asking me crazy questions about the show—you know, whether Sheree and Kim and I would ever be cool again, if I could tell them where I bought one of the tops I wore on the show, or maybe where I'd gotten the birthday cake for the birthday party I had for my son. I did not, however, expect anyone to ask me about my past—that past.

Is it true you used to be an exotic dancer?

It was a shocker, for sure. There aren't a lot of people who know I danced. My hair was short and black back then. I remember that because when I danced in the second club, there was another dancer whose name was Silk, and so I changed my name to Holly, after Halle Berry, because my haircut was like hers back in the day. So random people who weren't paying attention wouldn't necessarily remember me because today my hair is short and brown and cut much differently. Whoever asked that question knew me for real, was someone in my inner circle who probably isn't a friend anymore. Someone privy to the details of my life.

I can answer questions just fine, even the shocking ones. But this one almost got the best of me. Almost. I figured out a way to get through it. I have a slick enough mouth and enough good sense to put some words together to answer the one question and get everybody to move on to the next one. Telling my fans that I strip every night for my husband made clear to whoever was putting my business out there that what I did for a living in my twenties was as private to me as what happens in my bedroom with my man. I may give you a tidbit or two to chew on, but the rest really isn't any of your business. I felt that way while I was dancing. Except for Gregg, I never told anyone, not even potential suitors I was kickin' it with, that I was a stripper. They didn't need to know what I did at my day job because I only told people who really got to know me, and of the few guys I talked to during the three years I danced, Gregg was the only one who seemed like he was really interested in getting to know *me*. So I told him—he deserved to know. But unless you were close to me, I wasn't just going to tell you all my business. I didn't care if I was stripping or running a Fortune 500 company, it wasn't anyone else's concern.

That's how I felt about it.

I'm not ashamed that I danced. But I think it's important that women—particularly young women—understand *why* I danced. First, you should know that I'm by no means ashamed of my game. What difference does it make if I danced or not? Is the sun going to stop shining? Is my past taking food out of *your* mouth? I'm not embarrassed; hell, everybody at the AU Center was dancing. I had two of the best reasons in the world to do it, too: for the sake of my son, and to restore my confidence in myself. My child could live the good life, and I could build up the power I'd lost at the hands of my abuser. My ability to dance over a big, strong, strapping man and watch him grow so damn weak that he'd keep digging in his pocket and pulling out hundreds just to *look* at me was a real power trip. I'd been slapped and belittled and stomped on and disrespected countless times by a man, but all I had to do was slap my own ass and show him my goodies to make him powerless—over himself and his wallet. I had no problem making them feel like shit, too. If I didn't want to dance for him, I wouldn't, and I'd tell him, in the harshest way I could, so he'd feel low. "What? Seventy-five dollars is not enough for you to see these titties," I'd say. "I can go on to the next guy and get a hundred and fifty. Save those pennies for the next chick."

And I could keep my dignity intact collecting $150 from the next guy, and go home and sleep like a baby, knowing that I was stripping for all the right reasons.

That was powerful to me.

And guess what? If I had it to do all over again, I wouldn't change a thing. Not. One. Thing. I would take the same path because had I not, I would not be where I am today. I can't say I would take it all back. I am stronger today because of it. I am wiser today because of it. And I still don't see dancing in the club as a bad thing. I didn't have fights in there, everybody in the clubs liked me, I didn't do anything to disrespect my body, and I came out just fine.

But I will tell you this: You couldn't pay me enough to do it again. Oh, the opportunity has presented itself. Kim kept telling me that she was looking to pose in *Playboy*, and asked me once or twice if I would do it with her. I mean, every damn week, Kim was going to be posing for *Playboy*, like it was her life's dream or something. I haven't seen her up in that magazine yet, not sure if she was really invited to spread her goodies all over the pages or if she was hoping someone from *Playboy* would call her. But I know one thing: I wasn't about to pose with her ass.

Come on now: How would I look at my age, with a teenage son and a ten-year-old, all laid out in *Playboy*? All I would need is for one of Brice's friends to walk up to him with the magazine in his hands and say to my child, "Look at your mama." That would kill me. It really would. He's old enough now to understand it, and old enough to be hurt by the judgment people would pass on his mother. He was a baby back then, but not now. And I simply couldn't put him in the position of having to defend my decisions.

I also would never dance again because obviously, I know better. I know that there were so many other things I could have done—so many other options I could have considered—when I was trying to figure out how to raise my son the way I wanted to raise him. The one thing I didn't have back then was a parent talking to me and guiding me and caring about what I was doing. If I had it, I sure didn't know it. My aunt wasn't calling and saying, "Nene, we'll help you take care of Brice" or "Nene, I got some money for you." I simply didn't have that support, and I had to do everything—pay someone to watch him if I wanted to go out, buy the groceries, pay the rent and the light bill, make sure the car was working and the insurance was paid for. My son's father wasn't kicking in on any of the bills; hell, he lived in the inner city, in the slums. I wanted my child to be as far away from that as possible, for him to have a life that was better than the one I had coming up.

And now, I work hard to keep Brice from making the same mistakes I did. He's nineteen, not too far from the age I was when I fell into the arms of an abusive man and became a single mom and had to figure out how to make it on my own. You saw on the show how much I'm in my son's business. But you know what? That's what he has a mother for. I'm supposed to help guide and advise him so that he doesn't make the same mistakes I did, and when he becomes a father, he should be in the position of doing the same thing for his children. So if my child needs me to help him buy a car so he can get to his job that I helped him get, so that he can go to school or have a little money in his pocket, that's what I'm going to do. I didn't have any business signing a lease with no job when I was in my twenties, but if my child decides he wants to live on his own, I'm going to make sure that he finds an apartment he can afford and that is safe, and that he understands how credit works so that when he gets older, he'll actually have some.

Most important, he's going to know that he has someone in his corner, and that he is loved.

Chapter 8

BAD BOYS WILL GET YOU NOWHERE, ESPECIALLY IF THEY MAKE YOU SLEEP ON MR. RIGHT

On our first date, Gregg showed up to my town house with flowers and chocolates in the backseat of the car, dressed like an OG—had on gator shoes, slacks with the big cuffs and the wide legs, and a front license tag that read, "Strictly Business." When we left for our date, he opened the car door for me and stood outside of it like he was a chauffeur.

It was so wrong on so many levels for me, at least at that time, because it seemed like he was trying way too hard and using win-her-over tactics my uncle might have used on my aunt when they started dating in the backwoods of Georgia, way back in the 1940s. I mean, I was in my late twenties, independent and fly, and here was this older guy showing up for the first date looking and acting like he'd gotten his dating cues from a dusty turn-of-the-century "courting" manual. The OG thing was a chemistry killer for me, for sure—and if I didn't have chemistry with the man standing in front of me, it didn't matter how cute he was or what gifts he brought me or what he was whispering in my ear. If I wasn't feeling him, he wasn't going to be "feeling" me—period.

I'm picky like that.

But Gregg? He was persistent, not easily cowed, from the giddyup. I met him through a mutual friend at the Martini House over in Buckhead, a cute little spot where ballers went to drink martinis and smoke cigars. I'd just gotten off work, and my girls, who were there having cocktails, called me to join them. I didn't even bother dressing up; I hadn't intended on staying long. I didn't even have a drink, just went there to say hello right quick and then get on home to my baby boy.

But, as fate would have it, I spotted my friend Willie across the way and I sashayed over to his table to say hello and kick it with him for a few minutes before I headed for the door. Gregg was sitting with him; I was cordial, of course, a lady. And before I excused myself from our brief conversation, I tossed Gregg a compliment: "Oh, those are some nice shoes."

Of course, I went on about my business, giggling with my girls and being Nene. I must have made quite an impression, because before I knew it, Willie was standing next to me, talking about "My friend wants your number."

"Oh, no," I insisted. "I just like his shoes. Really, I'm not interested."

"Go ahead and give the man your number, baby, it's no big deal—let him take you out. He's a good guy," Willie insisted.

Now, I kept some fake numbers stored away in my mind for occasions just like these, when men I wasn't interested in couldn't and wouldn't take no for an answer. But for some crazy reason that I can't recall right now, I gave the man my *real* phone number.

He called me for weeks, kept leaving messages on my answering machine. "Hey, call G!" "Give G a call!" "It's G, call me!" God, I thought it was the most annoying thing to come home and find yet another message from a man I had no interest in talking to or seeing.

Until one night when I got into a disagreement with my sister, with whom I'd been staying. Genesis, you see, had moved back to Alabama, and I didn't want to stay at the place we'd shared together, so my sister, who'd lived with me when she first moved down from Queens to Athens, returned the favor by letting me stay with her while I found a new town house for me and my son. I don't even remember what we were arguing about. I just didn't want to argue with her anymore and needed to get the hell out of the house and far away from her mess. So I ran through my phone book trying to find someone to hang out with that night. I tried my fun girlfriends and my not-so-fun friends, too—folks I'd seen recently and people I hadn't seen in a minute. I even called this guy I was kind of talking to at the time. He wasn't anybody serious, just some guy I'd let take me out on a date or two, and talk on the phone with every now and then. As fate would have it, none of my friends were around—not one. So I said to myself, "Let me call Big Daddy."

And when he heard my voice on the other end of the phone, asking him if he wanted to go somewhere, that fool didn't hesitate for one minute. He was like, "YES!"

Even the way he answered immediately, I didn't like. There was no, "Well, wait, let me check my schedule" or "Oh, I have plans but maybe tomorrow." None of that. Just an overeager "YES!"

Ugh.

COULD THIS BE LOVE?

I'll tell you this much: That first date was the best date I'd ever had. He took me to a Japanese steak house, a restaurant experience I'd never had before. We sat at the bar and had a few drinks and talked about everything under the sun, and when we finally got seated, we were so engrossed in each other that we didn't even notice that the table where we were sitting was full of strangers. He ordered my dinner for me and kept the conversation flowing. He was obviously smart and interesting, mature, down-to-earth, and sweet. He wasn't materialistic, but he liked nice things, had taste.

I liked that.

And when our date was over, he asked me if he could take me out the next day. I accepted, telling myself that "Big Daddy"—the nickname I secretly called him because he had money and was older than me—would make the perfect "cool lunch buddy." Later, after I moved into my own place—almost an hour away from his house in Lithonia—I put him through the paces I always put guys through when they called themselves liking me: I gave him "the List."

Oh, trust. How a guy responded to the List told me everything I needed to know about his ass, in particular, whether he was really down for Team Nene, or if he was trying to use me for his "needs" and then be gone. The way it worked was like this: If a man used my digits and invited himself over, I'd tell him he could come, but only if he stopped at the store and picked up a few things for me on the way. When I was a teenager, I dated a guy who worked at Kentucky Fried Chicken, and he knew he couldn't come see me after he got off work if he didn't bring a bucket over with him. And when I first started working at the club, a man named Ziggy called himself trying to get in, and I told him if he wanted to come see the kid, he needed to bring some pull-ups, a bag of Lay's, a 2-liter of Coke, and some Ritz crackers.

"But it's storming outside," he said. "You really want me to stop at the store?"

"If you're coming over, you need to work with my list," I insisted.

He didn't feel like going to the store and picking up what I needed, so he couldn't come over to my house and get what he needed. Simple as that. (Oh, and don't get your panties all in a bunch—I'm not talking about exchanging crackers and soda for sex. When I say that "get what he needed," I mean that he could earn the privilege to spend time with me—nothing more, nothing less.)

Gregg got a helluva list the first time he got ready to

make his way to my new apartment. I'd just moved in and I needed the essential things you need when you're in a new place and you're starting fresh.

"Well, if you're going to come over, you need to bring a mop, a broom, some washing powder, a bag of rice, an onion for this spaghetti, and a few other things, too," I insisted.

Now, that man said he was going to come over and bring me what I needed. But wouldn't you know it? He stood me up! He didn't come by the house that night or bring me the things I told him to bring. And wouldn't you know it? I still let him back in. Maybe because he offered to take me out to a nice dinner and gave me the money for what I needed. Or maybe it was because he made clear he wasn't trying to play any games with me, that while some loser would be happy to get over with buying a broom and a mop and an onion and then think that was all he was obligated to do, Gregg was the type of guy who was thinking bigger picture. He made up for ignoring my list by knocking off a few things on a much bigger list—like the light and gas bills, the tuition, and the rent. And his admiration and love. Yup, he was crazy enough to do it.

It never even crossed my mind, though, that I'd met the man I was going to marry. Funny thing is, Gregg knew it from jump. He used to say all the time, "One of these days, you're going to be my wife." I'd just look at him like he was a stone nut and laugh. Wasn't no way. I mean, this man was just coming out of a marriage—had put a ring on her finger when he was eighteen and stayed married to her for twenty years. They had five children together, and he had been raising three of them by himself during their three-year separation. And though they'd gone their separate ways and she was in a new relationship with another man, the divorce wasn't final yet. Gregg was the antithesis of what I wanted in a mate. I wanted someone around my age who had never been married and didn't have a bunch of kids—because I wanted my husband and me to experience marriage for the first time together, and I didn't want a team of kids and ex-wives and baby mamas to get all up in our love mix.

It wasn't until my aunt met Gregg that I nixed my reservations about building a lasting relationship with him. Getting them together wasn't easy, mind you. It was Thanksgiving, and I wanted him to come with me to Athens to her big holiday feast, but he kept refusing. He was scared, you see, because he'd been married and had five kids and he was convinced that my old-school aunt would frown on him for that. So I ended up riding out to Athens by myself, pissed that Gregg had begged out of the festivities.

"Where's your friend?" my aunt asked as she hugged me and pulled me into the house.

I hesitated to tell her because I didn't want to have to explain the whole wife and kids thing to her. I knew, too, that she wouldn't care for all of that—that she would think it a lot of baggage for me to take on after coming through the storms I'd pulled myself out of. But I told her anyway, about the wife and the kids and the reason why he didn't want to come to Thanksgiving dinner. To my surprise, she didn't say anything about it except, "He should have made this trip."

Well, wouldn't you know it? About an hour after I arrived, he came on and brought his ass to Athens! I was shocked when he knocked on the door—shocked and happy, because I really wanted him to be there, and there he was. He sat down next to my aunt and she talked to him and loved him.

They hit it off just fine. And later, my aunt pulled me to the side and talked to me about him and the wife and the kids, pointed out that it wasn't like he had a bunch of kids with a bunch of different women, or that he couldn't be serious about marriage because his first marriage didn't work. "That man was married for nineteen years," she said. "They had a really long run." And when she finished talking to me about him—finished making me understand how special his former relationship was and what that said about him as a man and a husband and a father—I knew that it was okay for me to love him.

MY GUY

After that, we were going steady—I was his girl, he was my man. And we were damn near inseparable, enjoyed each other's company and comfort, listened to each other's joys and fears, and, slowly but surely fell in love.

Thing is, I was keeping that huge secret from Gregg, the one about being a stripper. I had him thinking I worked a regular nine-to-five somewhere stable, and the longer we dated, the harder we fell for one another, the guiltier I felt about not telling him the truth. I loved him. I wanted to build a life with this man who'd shown me nothing but kindness and love from the moment he'd laid eyes on me. I didn't want this one to get away. But I knew that if our relationship was to go where I wanted it to—toward a serious, lifelong commitment—I had to tell this man the truth about what I did for a living to support myself and my young son. I just couldn't lie to him anymore.

I guess I also needed to know for sure if he truly loved me, regardless of what I did for a living. Up until that point, Gregg and I had shared a lot about our lives—our faults, our mistakes, our hopes, our fears. And he rolled with all the punches, listened to and comforted me when I told him about my upbringing and my abusive relationship. He never judged me. Never pointed fingers. And always offered sound advice about how I could move on, get on with my life. And he made clear that he wanted me to do that with him.

But what man can really handle that his girlfriend gets naked in front of a bunch of other men? Sure, they don't mind going to strip clubs to watch someone else's woman take off her clothes. But actually knowing *your* girl takes off her clothes for other men? I figured if he could get over that? He was a helluva guy.

So I told him.

He didn't believe me, thought I was pulling his leg, trying to play a trick on him. I kept telling him I was dead serious, but he didn't stop laughing and challenging me on it until I pulled out my work bag, the one with my costumes and makeup and garter belt and stilettos. "I'll tell you what," I said. "Come down to the club and see if you don't believe me."

He got quiet for a minute, lost in his thoughts. I couldn't tell what was on his mind, how he was feeling about the situation. If he still thought I was kidding, or if he was trying to figure out a way to make a hasty exit. Finally, he said simply, "I'll stop by."

He came through, stepping in there with sneakers and a jersey, trying to look hip and cool and younger than he was. I could tell this wasn't his scene. He seemed uncomfortable, and it was clear he was burying himself in his drink to keep from looking at the dancers. He was no match for Silk, though, I sauntered over to him and put my hand on his shoulder. "Want a dance?" I cooed softly. He grinned a sly grin, and nodded. And then I proceeded to throw it on him like I've never thrown it before.

When I finished, he told me I looked hot—and he tipped me, too.

And then he had his talk with the manager, and the rest of our relationship story is history.

Gregg's proposal came within a year of that first date when he showed up to my place in his OG car. Check out how it happened. I'd been planning to buy myself a new car, and he'd gone with me to a dealership a few days earlier to check out some rides when I came across this beautiful cherry red BMW that I absolutely fell in love with. It was more than I could afford, though, and so I left the car there and continued my search. What I didn't know was that Gregg went behind my back and worked out a deal with the owner and bought the car for me. A few days later, he called me on the phone, talking about how he knew I really liked the car and that I should take a quick test-drive in it to see if it was worth trying to talk the owner into giving me a deal. "Okay," I said. "Come through and pick me up."

Before I knew it, Gregg and I were speeding down 1-20, headed for his house, riding in that red 325 BMW. I was admiring the handle when he asked me if I *really* liked the car.

"Oh, yes," I said. "This car is *bad*."

"This car is also yours," he answered back.

"What?" I exclaimed. "Mine?"

Turns out Gregg had purchased the car for me. It was incredible. Gregg was the first guy ever to do things like that for me, who made me feel pretty and took me out on real dates and bought me real gifts like cars and expensive bags and jewelry. It was the best thing ever for a young girl like me to have a guy buying me that luxury car. But that BMW wasn't just any gift, now. Nope, it was much more. It was an engagement gift! As we made it down the highway, he turned to me and said simply, "We ought to get married."

"For real? You want to marry me?" I smiled.

"Yeah," he said. "Go ahead and plan your wedding."

The proposal wasn't mushy. There was no getting down on one knee or finding my favorite sunrise or taking me to my favorite restaurant or any "Will you marry me?" scrawled across the sky. It was just Gregg and me, making a very grown-up decision to take our relationship to the next level. We'd been dating for a year, and I'd made it clear to him that a year was all the time we'd need to figure out if we were right for each other, all the time we needed to decide if we were going to stay together or let each other go.

I realized that this man was quality, that he was good to me and good for me, and truly loved me, flaws, abrasive ways, larger-than-life personality and all. He was responsible, smart, and attentive, had good conversation, and would sooner chop his own hands off than raise a finger to hurt me. And he was a fantastic provider, took great care of those kids as a single dad. His two oldest children—twins—had already graduated from high school and were out on their own by the time Gregg and I started dating, but he was fully in charge of the other three, a second grader, a middle schooler, and a high schooler. He got them ready for school, helped with homework, cooked dinner, bought their clothes, all of that. He was sensitive, about introducing women to them, even me. Indeed, for a long time while we dated, they never met me. If I spent the night at his house, I'd come in after his children were sleeping, and I'd stay in his room while he got them ready and out the door in the mornings, and none of them would be the wiser. After we got serious, he planned a barbecue with just him, me, and the kids, so that they could meet me and we could start to get to know each other. It went well—they were good, nice kids. And once I'd totally fallen in love with Gregg, I got myself pumped up to raise those kids, to take them in and do for them like my aunt did for me and my brother when our mother wasn't around.

Now don't get me wrong—it wasn't easy. By then I was in my late twenties with a second grader, and there I was about to help bring up three more kids. The boys were easier; they'd do boy stuff with Bryson, and so they were occupied and relatively happy. It was harder on his daughter, though, because she was the only girl and she was a teenager going through the awkward teen years and, really, she wanted her mom around. I could relate to that. I felt the same way about my mom when I was her age, that's for sure.

We tried to make it work. I even convinced Gregg that we should move to a different house from the one he was living in, the house that he'd shared with his first wife. I wanted to start fresh, so that all of us would feel like we were moving on together toward something new. We got the house all right, and even moved into it. But about a month before the wedding, the kids started to get antsy and calling for their mother's attention. One weekend, out of the blue, she picked them up for a visit and never brought them back to us.

Of course, Gregg was extremely sad about it. Those were his babies, and for years he had raised them and tended to their needs exclusively. But if I'm going to be honest, I have to come clean on it: Physically, I was prepared to make the transition to stepparent, but my mind was telling me, "Oh, thank you, Jesus—she didn't bring them back!" I couldn't do it, and I knew I wouldn't be able to. I wasn't in any kind of mood to raise four kids—I mean, come on!

Today, I get along with his kids just fine, and after almost twelve years that we've been married, I can truly say that he is wise and loving, a terrific father to both of my sons—the one who is his by blood and the one whom he accepted as his own child from the get-go—and still, after all these years together, in love with me.

And I, after all these years, love him still, too. I picked well. We both did. And I'm glad we said, "yes." I can't guarantee that we'll be together forever—like every other couple, we certainly have our issues and some days it's harder to make it work than others. But at least we're trying.

THIS I KNOW FOR SURE

You could have told me a thousand times that the man I complimented at the Martini Bar was going to be my husband, and I would have told you two thousand times that you were out of your damn mind. He wasn't anything like the ideal guy I'd envisioned in my mind. He wasn't young, he wasn't hip, he wasn't fly. He was just a regular guy, but with bank. I'm not going to lie. That he was a businessman with money certainly didn't hurt his chances with me. But at the end of the day, he simply didn't fit into the mold of the guy I *thought* I wanted.

What was I looking for, you ask? Superficial stuff, really. I wanted a guy who was flashy and who smelled good, cared about clothes and cars and was tall and had curly hair. I wanted him never to have been married. because I wanted my future husband to experience that with me for the first time.

I wasn't thinking about the things that matter in a relationship, the things that would change my life for the better, for real. It took me a minute to figure out that what I needed from a man extended far beyond the superficial things, far beyond what would impress my girls, or would push me to my limits. Stability—this is what I needed.

But I hadn't a clue what that looked like. My father wasn't around, so I didn't know what traits to look for in a good daddy. I knew what I didn't want, but I barely knew what I *did* want. I'd had only one serious relationship before I met Gregg, and that one was explosive—full of abuse, disappointment, frustration, dishonesty, and fear—so I didn't know what to expect from a good boyfriend/husband.

Gregg stepped in and showed me the vision. He cared deeply for my son. He doled out plenty of hugs and high fives, encouragement and praise and discipline, too. And he made clear that even though he had five children from his previous marriage, he wanted to be in my son's life, and maybe one day even have a child with me, a baby we could raise together. A child made out of love *and* loved.

Most important, though, Gregg took care of me. He loved me beyond measure and then did everything within his power to make sure I was happy. I wanted for nothing with him. In addition to the little things—opening doors, taking me to the finest restaurants, lavishing me with great gifts, constantly professing his love for me, doing sweet, unexpected things like serving me breakfast in bed and taking Bryson and me on fabulous trips—he stepped up big-time for the things that mattered. He made a beautiful home for me and my son. He worked hard, paid the bills, and brought his money home where it belonged. And he was trustworthy and honest and wise, even beyond his years. His curly hair and dark chocolate skin were a bonus.

I'm not saying I had low expectations or standards for what I wanted in a guy, and I'm certainly not saying that Gregg is perfect. Oh, he's got a flip side. He's very headstrong and it seems to me that the older he gets the more our likes and wants and needs go in opposite directions. Like my dream is to travel the world one day, to explore all of the beautiful countries and cultures and people I've admired from afar and always wanted to see up close. He doesn't seem to have any interest in doing this. And he's much grouchier, too, particularly now that I'm in the entertainment business. The business is very hard on Gregg; he's used to me being home and taking care of the kids and tend-ing to things—being a wife and a mother. A week can go by easily without him and the kids seeing me because I'm out on the road, filming the show or making appearances, and when I get home, I'm too tired to cook and clean like normal people do. Hell, we can't even go out for a bite to eat without being interrupted by someone looking for an autograph or a conversation—and he can't stand that. It's not an easy thing to be married to someone in the business, especially if you're not a part of it.

Of course, all of this just makes Gregg and me a normal couple, with ups and downs and highs and lows and joy and pain and good and bad. What we've been through, and what is still to come, is no indication of whether we're capable of staying together or we're headed for splitsville. Like everyone else, our marriage simply is.

Still, my husband and children are the most important people to me, and my point in writing this is to make clear that it was a mistake to limit my choices in men. If I hadn't opened my heart to the possibilities, I might have missed out on a great guy. It turns out that what Gregg lacked initially in the chemistry department, he more than made up for with true love, the kind of love that is healthy and pure and worth a second look. And I'm glad I took that look. Because now I know not to judge a book by its cover—to flip through the pages, feel its weight in my hands, and read beyond the title page to see whether someone is worthy of my time and attention.

You should try this, too—or risk the same mistake I almost made by missing the diamond in the rough.

Chapter 9

FINDING A NEW WAY TO LOVE

Most everybody has one in the family—you know, the older lady who's tough as nails and full of wisdom, and knows instinctively how to make everything all better with a big plate of homemade Southern delicacies like pigs' feet and hog maws and those heavy lemon butter pound cakes. She takes great pride in being no-nonsense, is an expert at swooping down a tree branch for wayward kids who dare get out of line, and doles out hugs and "I love yous" on special occasions only, because anything more is a frivolous expenditure of energy—particularly when you should know that she loves you all right but is much too busy/uncomfortable/devoid of skilled emotion to actually show it. At least in that huggy, touchy-feely way they do in the movies and on *The Cosby Show*. Nope, won't be any kissing and pretty words. Not from her. Just no-nonsense, tell-it-to-you-straight, disciplined child rearing.

In my family, this person is my aunt, the woman who took me in when I was a baby and raised me like I was her own. Though my aunt had a daughter from a previous relationship, she and my uncle never had any children together, and so it made sense that the two of them became very attached to Anthony and me when they convinced my mom to let us stay with them. And together, they gave us the life our mother didn't have in herself to give us. It was my aunt who had the biggest hand in our raising. And trust me when I tell you: Nena Thomas, affectionately known as Nellie to everyone who knows her, was—and still is to this very day—no joke. She drank coffee every day and smoked cigarettes and talked really loud, in a voice that could carry all the way down the block, take a left, and wake the neighbor a couple streets over. She's loud, for sure. Say something to her about it and she'll tell you quick, fast, and in a hurry it's your problem, not hers. "I'm not yelling. I just talk loud," she insists. She's old school, I promise you. Past old school, really. She's in her eighties, and if you walk up on her with the foolishness, she will tell it to you straight, right there, right now. I appreciate that about her; it's probably where I got it from. She raised me, so it makes sense.

I am, of course, grateful to her for rescuing me and my brother when it seemed like our mom was falling down on her parental duties. She gave me a roof over my head. She put clothes on my back and food in my stomach. When I needed to see the doctor or the dentist, it was she who took me. When I needed to go to school, she registered me, and when I got the notion in my head that I was going to be a model/actress/dancer/ famous, she indulged me by paying for modeling school and dance lessons and the fees I needed to participate in all the sports and after-school programs I signed up for. She was there for all the milestones—my first step, my potty training, my first day of kindergarten, my high school graduation. When I needed a little spending money, it was my aunt who put it in my pocketbook.

Aunt Nellie was there for me.

She led by example, too. She worked hard, first as a cook at a frat house over at the University of Georgia, and later as a seamstress, whipping up fabulous window treatments for the locals in her native Athens. And everybody came to my aunt's house for her big holiday dinners. Thanksgiving and Christmas were a big deal at her place, and she would go all out for us. She gave us everything—every toy and every game we saw on TV and thought we'd like, mounds of cute outfits we picked out of the pages of the Spiegel catalog, shoes, the works. And on Christmas Day, every branch on the huge tree she centered in the living room would be lit with a light, bright as can be. And on the table? Oh, man, the table would be stacked with homemade goodies, you hear me? She could cook! In fact, she cooked every day. Country breakfasts with eggs and ham and biscuits made from scratch, with the flour and the biscuit cutter and everything. She made real dinners every night, too. She was famous for her fried chicken—she'd do drummettes—and everybody knew when we were having a cookout, you better come with an empty stomach because my aunt aimed to fill your belly with all kinds of Southern delicacies, from pig tails and chitterlings to barbecued ribs to fried fish and macaroni and cheese and potato salad.

Yeah, my aunt knew how to make it special.

SHE AIN'T NO JOKE

As much as I appreciate what my aunt did right for me, there were a lot of things she did wrong, too. She wasn't caring or affectionate. At. All. I wish she could have been a little softer around the edges, understood that children need more than just things. That we need to feel and be told that we are loved. Like my mom, my aunt never really said those three special words, never showed it in any great way. In fact, she was quite hard on me and my brother, strict as any old-school mom could get. She did what most good parents do—she gave us allowances and rules and curfews, and I understand the need for those things. But boy, if my brother and I stepped outside of the boundaries she created? Whoa. If we went out and she expected us back at a certain time, we'd better be back when she said be back—go straight home, don't even look at anyone else's house, let alone stop by there to kick it for a minute. I couldn't date until I was sixteen, and even then it was a situation. There was no talking on the phone to girls she didn't like and especially boys, and especially after a certain time of the evening. She would listen in, too, honey—pick up on the other end and embarrass the mess out of me if she didn't like what she was hearing or the time at which she was hearing it. "Didn't I tell you not to be on this phone at such and such a time?" she'd fume into the phone. "Hang it up right now!"

Whoo. I'd be too embarrassed to go to school.

And if you violated even the tiniest, most simple rule, get ready for the wrath. She would put us on punishment in a heartbeat, you hear me? And your ass would stay on punishment until it was over and done with, down to the minute. If she said at 6:32 P.M. on Tuesday that you can't see the light of day for the next week? Best believe you weren't going to look out the damn window again until next Tuesday at 6:32 P.M., period. She might just tear your little ass up while she was at it, too. Back then, you see, you got whippings, and the kind of whippings we got would be considered abuse today. They don't let you do all that shit today. We had to go outside and get that switch, and she would tear you up, my aunt. No amount of crying, begging, pleading, promising, or screaming was going to save your ass. When she got it in her mind that you needed your butt beat, she beat that ass.

I didn't get too many wallopings growing up. I did what I had to do to avoid them. But my brother? He got one practically every day. He was a trip like that. But if we were walking home from school and my aunt said come straight back when classes are over, I'd be like, "Uh-uh, she said to be there by 4:30 P.M., and I'm going to be there by 4:30 P.M. because Nene is *not* getting hit, honey."

But even worse than the strict discipline was my aunt's absence. She just wasn't there for me, you know? She was always working and so she couldn't be at the school and be involved in a whole lot of the things I was doing to better myself as a student, athlete, and up-and-coming performer. I had a lot of friends whose parents worked, and somehow they managed to be there for their daughters when it counted. She never came to my basketball games, never watched me get my groove on in the cheerleading squad, barely made it to any of my pageants.

Indeed, going to the pageants alone was the worst, because the intimacy of the behind-the-scenes experience lent itself to the contestants depending on their parents for help with everything. There were gowns and shoes to purchase and hair and makeup to be done and talent to be shown, and practically every girl had a parent behind the scenes, helping her into her wardrobe changes, and fussing with her hair and eye shadow, and encouraging her as she made her way to the stage, and especially when she hadn't performed well. I watched them while I did my own hair and my own makeup and struggled into my gown, eyed them while I sat in the corner, wishing my mom or my aunt were there to pat me on my hand and tell me, "It's going to be all right. You were great, but it's okay if you don't win. We're proud of you anyway."

It made me so incredibly sad to have to do it alone. And it made me feel odd. Like I wasn't loved.

ON MY OWN

It didn't feel any better once I got older, either. In fact, it was more glaring. I guess because I became more aware as a young adult that I was living life without knowing the rules that count. My aunt was a stickler for making sure we did our chores and made it home when she said to be home and didn't talk all night on the phone, but she never taught us how credit works, or how to pay a bill, or how to sign a lease or make a major purchase. She wasn't there to help me get my first apartment, to help me figure out what I could afford, or to say, "Okay, if you want to make this rent on time, you have to put aside this certain amount of money every check so that you can pay your bill." She didn't tell me when I was about to make my first car purchase what was a good deal and what was a sucker's bet. She didn't teach me the rules of dating a guy or give me any sound advice about sex. She just said don't date and don't have sex. The guidance, basically, was nonexistent, and when I got of a certain age, it was, "All right, then, you're of age, you're on your own. Now you figure that out." There were no offers to help. Nothing. In fact, I can remember clear as day the first time I ran back to Athens, my ex hot on my heels, threatening to give me another beating worse than the one he'd just finished meting out. I went to my aunt in confidence, scared and confused and desperate for some kind of advice on how to get out of the mess I'd gotten myself into.

"He's been hitting me," I said, tears welling in my eyes.

My aunt just looked at me and shook her head a little, said a few choice words, and went on back to what she was doing. I don't remember the specific words she said to me, but I do know how those words made me feel as they tumbled from her lips: I felt lower than low, like she was blowing off what I'd just told her and, to some extent, suggesting that I actually deserved to be beat. She didn't respond the way a parent should respond when I told her I was in an abusive relationship. She didn't say, "Don't ever talk to him again" or "He says he won't hit you again, but he will, and you need to leave that relationship right now." In fact, she didn't say a whole lot of anything. Maybe she thought she shouldn't have anything to say about it, that it wasn't her place to get in the middle of my affairs. But I needed her. I needed her to be the adult, to shine a light and help me walk the path away from the abuse and toward a healthier relationship.

She didn't. Wouldn't.

Maybe that was because she, too, struggled with abuse in her own marriage. I don't think she recognized it as abuse, but today I sure can. My uncle Bobby was married to my aunt for many years before he passed away a few years ago of pancreatic cancer. Their time together is, for sure, a testament to long-lasting love. But they had an explosive relationship, and I don't think my aunt had a clue about how their fighting weighed on me, how his outrageous antics during his alcohol binges would forever taint my relationships with men and my kids.

My uncle, you see, was a quiet man, really nice and genteel. He didn't say much, hardly ever talked and never disciplined us. In fact, when my aunt got it in her mind to let us have it, he would say, "Leave them children alone!" He stopped us from getting many a spanking, I'll tell you that much. But if he got a little liquor in his glass, he would get drunk, and when he got drunk, my uncle would cuss my aunt out like you would not believe. He really was a trip; he'd be so loud and wrong with it, and my aunt would just sit here and take what he was dishing. Some days, he couldn't even walk; he'd be crawling all across the living room floor, screaming and calling my aunt all out of her name. He was a character, all right.

We could always tell when it was about to be on. He would call me over to the car and tell me to drive with him down to this bootleg liquor house he liked, and while I waited, he'd be in there getting his fill. And then he'd stumble on out and say, "Nene! Come over here and drive this car!" I didn't know thing one about driving, but I'd get on behind the wheel and put that car in gear and steer it on down the road. He'd stumble out of the car and get to crawling into the house on his hands and knees, and we'd laugh! My aunt would tell us to leave him alone, but I'd mess with him—put my hair bows in his hair. I got some pictures of that somewhere—him wearing my bar-rettes. I would say, "His ass is crawling around on the floor like a baby, he might as well have some hair bows!"

But we'd get really quiet when he'd catch sight of my aunt and lay into her. It was scary as hell to hear and see this sweet, genteel man roar like a madman, saying all kinds of ter-rible things to the woman he claimed to love and had been with forever. And she would yell and curse back at him—she wouldn't just take it. She was a tough lady, never backed down. But he was like Jekyll and Hyde—would be the kindest man when he wasn't drinking, but would turn into a stone-cold monster when that liquor hit his stomach.

Still, my aunt stayed with him. And loved him when he was sober. And enjoyed the good times until the next time he'd get drunk, and they fought again.

I look back on that and I realize that the man who ulti-mately ended up abusing me was just like that—a Jekyll and Hyde. Very sweet on the one hand, and crazy on the other. Ex-cept my ex didn't abuse with just words; he used his hands. And he couldn't blame alcohol for his mess. He just got off on beat-ing my ass, and he'd be sober as hell doing it. Still, I can't help but think that my uncle wasn't too much better than my abuser;

he didn't hit my aunt, but he abused her nonetheless. And I lived in the house with that and thought it was normal because nobody said or did anything to stop it.

It's just how it was.

But I know now just how wrong it was to grow up with that level of abuse, in a house devoid of emotion and true, affectionate love.

I know enough now to make sure that my house never devolves into that.

THIS I KNOW FOR SURE

I've thought about this a lot over the years, and I've finally come to the conclusion that my mom and her sister didn't say "I love you" or give affection because they never got it when they were growing up. Neither of them was capable of cloaking her children in the warmth that parents extend to their kids these days, because their parents never showed them how to. I don't think they knew how to be any other way but cold and distant. Their parents did them like that—practiced that "Children are to be seen, not heard" mantra, and my mom and aunt just gave to us what they got from their parents.

Personally, I think this is the story for all too many of us: We parent like we were parented, and if your mom and dad or whoever brought you up raised you in a way that scarred, you deal with the repercussions of those scars for a lifetime. Sometimes those scars manifest themselves in self-destructive behavior. Sometimes those scars rear their ugly heads in your relationships with others. And those scars can easily scab over the way you raise your own children, can make you yell at your kids constantly if you were yelled at constantly, or whip them if all you knew growing up was that hitting was the best discipline, or hold back emotion and affection if no one ever showed you emotion or affection when you were a child.

When I had my boys, I made the very conscious decision to try to do better by my kids than my aunt did by me, to raise them in a very specific way so that they would never feel the hurt I felt growing up and feeling unloved. Don't get it twisted: I did pick up some of my aunt's traits. I'm a yeller, for sure. If there were a Yellers Anonymous group somewhere, my ass would be sitting right there in the front row, talking about, "Hello, I'm Nene and I'm a yeller." I do it because my aunt did it, and because I have a loud, booming voice that carries—just like hers. I don't hit them—never have, never will—but I yell like a madwoman and warn them when I'm about to bust a gasket: "Listen! You are making me damn yell!" and "You got me yelling and shit, so stop it!" I understand, though, that raising my voice like that isn't good for them because it makes them nervous. And though Bryson, my oldest boy, is the quiet type, his little brother already is a screamer; I'm sure he gets it from me. So hey, I'm trying to dial it back. But when I do yell, I try to explain why I'm upset, and I make sure that my sons understand by the end of the conversation that I absolutely adore them, that my frustration is rooted in wanting the best for them and, especially, that it's cloaked in love. So instead of yelling, "Well, that was a stupid thing for you to do!" I'll tell my son, "Look, I'm mad about what you just did, but it's because I love you, I want the best for you, and I expect better from you." I'll tell my little

163

one, Brentt, why jumping off the banister isn't acceptable and how he could hurt himself if he keeps doing it, instead of just yelling at him for doing it.

Both of them know, because I tell them constantly, that there's a high price to pay if they don't listen to me, because I have the experience to give them the help they need. I've made the mistakes, and now I can hip them to the game so that they don't have to go through the things I went through to make it here. I tell them all the time that I know as teenagers they're going to go out there and make mistakes, that they're going to do things they shouldn't be doing. That's normal. But I'm not going to let them suffer through the huge mistakes. I will give them guidance to avoid them and a safety net in case they fall anyway. I didn't have these options with my aunt or my mother or any other adult in my life. I could count on them to criticize, that's for sure—they always had something to say about what I was doing. But help? Not so much. But I'll be damned if I don't do it different for my kids.

I'm not just talk when it comes to how I show my love to my sons. I recognize that my actions—showing them that I love them—are equally important. My aunt was always work-ing so I understand why she couldn't make it to a lot of the dif-ferent little shows and games and pageants and activities I was involved in. But she made no effort, either. In fact, I can re-member only one event she came to in all the time that I was involved in activities in junior high and high school, and that was to the Sweetheart Pageant, a popular Valentine's Day pag-eant held in Athens every year. I begged my mom and aunt to come—and to my surprise they agreed. My mother flew in from New York, and the two of them sat in the audience, smiling and laughing together and cheering me on. It meant the world to me. But that was the only time they were there, physically, for me.

I don't want my boys to grow up and say their mother rarely, if ever, came around for them. No matter how busy I am—and I stay busy, trust!—I make the time. I went with Bryson to help him buy his first car. It gave me great pleasure to help him find a vehicle, sit down with him at the dealer's desk and sign the papers with him, and hand over a stack to go toward the down payment. Buying his first car was a moment he'll never get back, and I was so happy I could be there for him to give him advice and help him out with a little something. My aunt didn't do that for me. And though Bryson hasn't moved out yet, I will help him secure his first place, too, another something my aunt didn't do. I look forward to it. I won't be paying his bills. But I will help.

I make a point, too, of being there for the little things. Something as simple as meeting Brentt at his school for lunch means the world to him. Now, I don't take any great pleasure in sitting there listening to fourth graders talk kid talk; what they're talking about makes no sense at all. I get up a little confused by the conversation but happy that I was there, because I know my son will remember that. I don't ever remember my aunt coming to my school to have lunch with me, and if I had asked, I imagine that she would have laughed me out of the room.

The funny thing about it is that my aunt is changing, too. My aunt never hangs up the phone without saying she loves me. She even tells me she misses me when I don't call for a few days. When she hears me yelling and punishing my kids when they do wrong, she'll say, "You have to explain to them why you're punishing them." And when she says that, I'm like, "Um, you didn't ever do that with us! Who are you right now?" In fact, she lets Bryson and Brentt get away with things she would have killed Anthony and me over for just suggesting them. Like the time she was keeping Bryson and tried to fix him oatmeal for breakfast. The boy had the nerve to tell her, "I don't even eat this—my mom doesn't make this!" If, when I was little, I turned my nose up at a bowl of oatmeal my aunt set in front of me at her table, do you know how many different ways I would have gotten laid out? But did she yell at Bryson? Oh, no! She took up his bowl of oatmeal and fixed him a whole 'nother breakfast! She was somewhere trying to make him happy. I cracked up when she told me that. "You did what?" I asked, incredulous. "In my house he would have been eating the oatmeal or wearing it." I laughed.

"You're too hard on him," she said. "All I did was whip up a couple of eggs for the boy. It wasn't a big deal."

So now she doesn't feel like yelling and punishing. She's in her eighties; maybe she's being nice so that she can get through the Gates. But I'll tell you this much, she's totally changed—in words and in actions.

And I'm doing what I can, too, to be a better parent.

My children deserve that much.

Chapter 10

LIGHTS, CAMERA, ACTION:
WATCHING YOURSELF ON TV IS
NOT FOR LIGHTWEIGHTS

*I*f you don't know, now you know: I love to run my mouth. Talking has always been a favorite pastime of mine. From the time I figured out how to push a word through my lips, I've loved to mix it up, get into people's heads, chat about nothing in particular and everything important—all with the hope that it would make me more knowledgeable, maybe lead to a few humorous moments or two, and, above all things, help give me a better understanding of why people do the things they do.

Sometimes, I even learn things about myself. And I'll tell you this much: I most definitely learned a lot about Nene during the taping of the first season—namely, that I really wasn't ready to run my mouth in such a public way.

When my family and I first got into the public eye, we didn't know what to say or how to act. We were stuttering and changing the way we talk, and being all kinds of awkward. A little proper. Like we were the damn cast of *Leave It to Beaver* and whatnot. I was June Cleaver in the middle of it all, trying to project myself as perfect and talk all proper and act like we were something other than what we are. I was listening to every word I said, trying to make sure I pronounced it correctly, and making sure I didn't sound Southern or illiterate. I wanted to sound right, you know?

It took only a few days of that, though, before I decided all of that June Cleaver mess wasn't going to work for me—for us. It was stressing me out. I was exhausted trying to make sure I said and did things specific to the image I was trying to project. Finally, I decided that the best thing for me to do was be me—to talk the way I talk and say whatever the hell I feel like saying and do what I normally do, and see how it turned out from there.

And you know what? Being real worked for me. That's how I got the reputation. Still, being in the public spotlight isn't easy. A lot of people on the outside looking in think it's easy, but it's hard and time-consuming and emotionally draining having people watch your every move all day every day, and making it hard to do even basic things like go to your son's school to have lunch with him because you're scheduled to do something else today, and you don't know when you'll be able to do that, actually.

It's difficult to be in the public eye, and expensive as hell, too. If I have four things to do in a day, I feel that I have to have four different outfits, and none of them can ever be worn twice, that's for sure. Hell, let me show up in the same outfit again and see how many stupid-ass people would get on their blogs, talking about, "Didn't she wear that already?" Like those people have pieces in their wardrobe that get worn one time and one time only. In my real life, I could buy a cocktail dress and wear it a few times. But now, once is all I feel I can get to wear my clothes, and sometimes I wear them for only a few hours because of what people may say. I might change my top a couple of times, and then throw on a dress for a lunch, and then in the evening wear a cute sweater and a different pair of slacks and stilettos. That's too much shopping, you hear me? In fact, Lisa and I have been plotting and planning to open up a store on eBay, so we can sell our closets. No use in us spending all that money and letting those clothes go to waste—that's hard cash, honey. That's not going to sit in my closet, I know that much. I need that money in my bank account.

In addition to the constant shopping, I pay someone to do my hair and makeup whenever I'm going out. That's another $200 to $250 *per day*, though the girl who helps me out gives me a small discount if she works for me on consecutive days. I'm paid, but I'm not about to give all my cash to the makeup lady. So if I need her four days out of the week, you do the math. I feel like I have to do it, though, because I want to look my best. Bet your bottom dollar she gives me a receipt, though, so I can write off all this M.A.C. and Bobbi Brown on my taxes.

EVERYBODY'S TALKING

Being a reality TV star is no joke. Definitely a whirlwind. I thank God they had someone taking pictures of us all the time, because if Bravo didn't have a photographer, we wouldn't have all of these memories. It happened so quickly it was hard for us to take it all in.

The reality of it all slapped me dead in the face the first time the show aired. I'll never forget that night. Bravo put out a thirty-minute sneak peek into the season and aired it at midnight for anybody who was willing to stay up and take it all in. I was in my bedroom, cuddled up with Gregg, the remote in one hand and my face in the other, peeking through my fingers at my image, larger than life. It was scary. I was looking at myself and judging myself. Oh, I hated it! I was a mess—my makeup didn't look right to me, my face was all shiny, and I thought I looked huge, like a plus-sized chick, even though in reality I'm only a size eight on a good day, a size ten when I have that extra slice of pie, sizes I consider average. I meet people all the time who check me on that, too. They'll say, "I didn't know you were that small" or "Girl, how'd you lose all that weight so fast?" They don't realize that the camera easily adds ten to fifteen pounds to your frame, so you have to be Nicole Ritchie/Angelina Jolie/ Kelly Ripa tiny to look even kind of normal on the TV. And don't let them shoot you from a weird angle or you'll be looking like a beached whale in purple Prada.

Not. Cute.

I knew from watching that little half-hour segment that the world was going to have something foul to say, and I wasn't sure I was ready for the onslaught. It's not like I could change anything. All of it was right there, laid bare for everyone to see and discuss and analyze and diss. Now, I had time to prepare for all of the buzz and gossip. I got to see the episodes a few days beforehand so that I could write my blog on Bravo and prepare myself for what everyone had to say about me.

Sure enough, the morning after the first show aired, the local radio shows, newspapers, and blogs were on fire. To hear them tell it, we were a gaggle of low-class, fake, hungry girls who were a disgrace to real housewives everywhere—particularly black ones. It was a mess! At first, the blogs and the comments and the stories bothered me, particularly because I'd never been in that situation before, where the masses could judge me and my actions in such a nasty, public way. But as time went on, and I acknowledged that everybody has an opinion and a right to it, the nastiness and vitriol stopped working my nerves. I quickly learned that the blogs were all run by a bunch of muthafuckas who ain't got nothing else to do, and soon enough my feelings stopped being hurt by what people were saying. Now none of it hurts my feelings. Nothing. I'm pretty tough, though, and a lot of stuff I don't read. My girlfriends might read something and if they think I should know about it, they'll tell me to check it out. But really, I don't have time to read what people say about me anyway. With my schedule and all the wonderful things I have going on, I hardly ever even get to see the computer. Mostly, I stay connected to my iPhone, and if I'm in the car service and not running my mouth or making the next deal, I can look up something I heard about really quick. But mostly, it's not worth the energy it would take to thumb in the website link.

Still, the show was real and a part of me. It made for a helluva show, I'll tell you that much, because we're all strong women, and we said exactly what we felt. That's when you have to have tough skin and let some of that shit roll off your back. It still hurt a little, though, to hear some of the things that were said about me, and it was particularly painful to watch myself say and do some things that I now wish I could do over.

For the most part, though, I'm happy with the way I was portrayed. Must have been, considering I signed up to do another season.

THIS I KNOW FOR SURE

I can't tell you how many girls come up to me and ask me how they can get on a show like *The Real Housewives of Atlanta*. They swear up and down that being on a show like ours will change their lives, that it'll be the end-all to their be-all. The game changer. But what those girls don't realize is that a lot of emotion and baggage come with having your life laid bare for all to see and judge and rip apart into tiny little shreds. People act like they know you for real after watching six episodes representing just six moments in your life, without considering that there's so much more to you, so much more that they didn't see. I get why people don't make the distinction. You can watch Will Smith in *The Pursuit of Happyness* and assume that the role he played was an act, that he's not really a homeless father-turned-millionaire, because he was portraying a role. But when people tune in to a reality show, they're assuming that what they're watching is, well, reality. And while what you saw of me on *Real Housewives* is real, it's only part of me that's real. It's my story, but it's not my complete story. There are many other facets to me.

The truth of the matter is that drama sells. No matter how much people claimed they were embarrassed by my in-your-face personality, they love to hear about my drama. Big-time. And over and over again. Nobody wants to see me going out and starting businesses, or having lunch with my kids, or cleaning the bathroom and cooking dinner. But I do these things. And anyone who says she cares to read about me doing those things is lying. Celebrities with no drama get no play, and they don't last. Period.

I understand the game, and I have no regrets about being on the show or how I was portrayed.

Not one.

In fact, I'm proud of what we accomplished and will forever appreciate all the benefits that came from it, particularly the memories. Sheree, Kim, DeShawn, Lisa, and I are forever connected because we had this experience together. We can look back on this as old ladies and say, "I did this show with these girls, and it was crazy and fun and eye-opening and incredible." I'd never claim any of these girls are my real friends. But we did get to share something special. And nothing—and no one—can ever change that.

You might find, though, that I'm a little different. I may not be so superloud, and I may dial back the beef I have with some of the other girls. I have definitely learned that not so many things need to be said out loud, that sometimes you have to bite your tongue and really think before you speak. Not only because I'm in the public eye but because I know that showing out like that doesn't become me. I've learned to bite my tongue just a little bit more, because sometimes it's for the best. Really it is.

But be clear: If a chick steps out of line, I'm still willing to put her in her place. I learned how to do this early in life—it's a part of my DNA—so it's not about to change.

That much you can bet on.

Chapter 11

STAY AWAY—FAR AWAY—FROM NUTS

I'm not sure if she's been clinically diagnosed, but I'm convinced that if she were to lie down on a doctor's couch, a psychiatrist would surmise within minutes that Kim is a wack job.

Let me paint a picture: I'd seen Kim around town—our kids went to the same camp, and occasionally we'd end up in the same stores, and seeing as both of us are larger than life, it was hard for us to miss each other. We'd say hi and such, but we didn't have any meaningful conversations until I saw her in the gym one day, working out with my trainer. She would come to the gym wearing those big-ass blond wigs she always wears, and had diamonds all on her fingers and arms and ears—dressed in a different Juicy Couture sweat suit every day of the week. And she'd hold court out in front of the gym like she owned the concrete it was laid on—always had a Louis Vuitton handbag at her feet and a cigarette dangling from her lips while she talked and laughed with that big, loud mouth of hers. I'd watch her and think, "She's, well, um . . . interesting." I'd never seen anyone like her before.

Anyway, when I found out we shared the same trainer, I decided to introduce myself. We chatted and clicked, and eventually we exchanged numbers. Some days later, she invited me over to her place after we realized we lived in subdivisions that were across the street from each other.

She was cool, you know? I didn't have any problems with Kim.

Kim and I would talk on an as needed basis; three or four weeks would go by before she returned a phone call. But when we got together, we'd have a lot of fun, you know? She's loud and free-spirited and clearly enjoys attention—that blonde who walks in a room and commands the attention of everyone in it. And the men? Yeah, the humongous boobs and the big fake hair and the trashy mouth and those flirty ways win them over every time. No doubt, by the time Hurricane Kim splits, men are left either mesmerized or drooling—sometimes both.

Kim just has that way about her.

That's how she ended up on the show. The producers had already said they were interested only in an African-American cast, but when a producer and I ran into Kim having lunch with her mom at the Clubhouse in Buckhead, she dazzled that producer so much, honey, by the time she left, she was thinking that Kim—clearly not a black girl—would be great for the show. I didn't try to stop it. I agreed that she's outgoing, funny, interesting, and probably would make for good TV, so I gave the producer her number and before I knew it, she was added to the cast.

But there's nothing to be fooled by: she's not a good friend. You have to go into a girlfriend relationship with her knowing that when you hook up with her, you'll have a great time—you'll laugh, you'll scream, you'll gossip, all of that—but the moment you walk off, she will talk about your ass like you were an enemy.

Nothing and especially nobody is ever good enough for Miss Kim. She is, without question, the most superficial person I have ever come across in my life. Nobody can give the looks she gives—the head-to-toe scan if Kim deems you don't have the money or class to hang with her. Labels are everything to Kim—Dolce & Gabbana, Gucci, Ferragamo, and all of that is a measure of your worth in her eyes, and if you don't have it, well, you're beneath her. Not worthy. A total loser.

And if Kim doesn't have labels and nice cars and an expensive home, she will literally die. I've never seen someone so doggone addicted to *things*. I've been in the store with this woman—watched her walk into Neiman Marcus and drop tens of thousands of dollars in not more than five minutes after she got herself through the door good. Hell, I've seen Kim buy a $20,000 bracelet just because it sparkles. She's literally addicted to spending money—and to anyone else who wastes cash like she does.

Gag me with two spoons and then take me to the river.

But Kim and me? Our friendship wasn't meant to be. I can't stand fake bitches like her, and she doesn't think I'm on her level, anyway. I don't boast and brag enough for her, refuse to wear my financial status on my clothing tags. Hell, if I'm wearing Dolce & Gabbana, I don't have to march up and down the street with a sign saying, "Look at me! I have on D&G!" I don't have to tell everyone within the sound of my voice, "Girl, you know I'm wearing Gucci, right?" If I'm looking nice, I don't need to tell you what it is I'm wearing—you'll get it. *I* make the designer, the designer doesn't make me.

Of course, I'm a girl, and what girl doesn't want nice things? I'm in the entertainment industry, so I have to look good at all times, and I like a designer bag and clothes and shoes just as much as the next chick—they're nice things to have and I like to have them. But D&G can kiss my ass—they're not getting all my money. You think I'm working all day to pay D&G? Please! Most people say they don't look at price tags, but you know what? I do. I shop on a budget—hell yeah, I do. We're in a recession and even if we weren't in one, I don't think it's smart not to pay attention to how much something costs. Shoot, I need to make sure it's worth every penny—I want to L.O.V.E. it and think about it and crave it before I bring it home. I will straight stalk an item before I hand over the ducats, for sure. Just recently, I went to the Gucci store to get an up-close look at this handbag I really wanted, and when I saw it, it just didn't move me, not for no $2,600. I wanted it to be bigger. I wanted it to make me say, "Damn, this hand bag is hot!" I just didn't feel that, and I walked out the store empty-handed and told myself that if I thought about it overnight and wished I had bought it, then I would go back and get it. Then I would know that I liked it, and I would be buying it because it was worth it. But Kim buys because she thinks designer things make her better!

Nene does not roll that way. My motto is, "If you don't love it, leave it." I'd much rather see the money I'd be dropping in those boutiques in my bank account, and know I can buy any of those things when I *feel* like it, not because I have to keep up with the Jone's. They're not getting my last dime, no ma'am. That's just not how I roll.

But Kim? Labels and the money it takes to get them *define* who she is. If you looked up and Kim was standing in front of you right now, she'd be dripping in designers down to her thong. Thing is, it's not *her* money she's spending on these things. She doesn't work—never has. Wouldn't know how to make a dime if you slapped her with a bucket of change. Every dollar that chick has is somebody else's money.

Correction: Somebody else's *husband's* money. She knows how to play second best. Damn shame, she thinks designer labels make her but they can't seem to get her a husband.

SECOND-PLACE CHICK

In the few years that I've gotten to know Kim, I've known her to date only married men. And they drop serious dollars on her— buy her homes and condos, jewelry, and clothes, expensive vacations. You saw her drive off the lot in a $60,000 car. That wasn't for play—that was how Kim rolls all day, every day, 365 days of the year. And every dime, as far as I've been able to see, comes from married men.

Which makes her the ultimate jump-off, doesn't it?

Well, I can testify that Kim's an excellent second-place chick. She plays her part well. She'll let her "boyfriend" sport his wife out on special occasions and play the left while the wife shines, and then hit up her man for baubles on the back end. Thing is, I don't think Kim's happy with this arrangement. I think that at the end of the day, she wants to be somebody's wife really bad. She even wears a wedding set on her finger, like she planned the wedding, invited the guests, and said, "I do" in front of God, her mama, and all her friends. She's a *great* second-place chick, but definitely not wife material. When she walks into the room, you can smell "single and desperate" on her, but when she's in public and gets around men? Honey, I don't know if it's the flirt in her, but she just doesn't look or act like the woman a man who's trying to have a family and make a stable home would want to get on bended knee for. Now if she would put some of those boobs away, stop being so flashy, calm down a little, get herself a good prescription, snatch that damn wig off, and wash that trashy mouth out, maybe a man might make her his wife.

Honestly, I think she's using her labels and her cars and her fancy town house and her relationships with married men to cover up something going on inside of her. I'm no psychiatrist so I can't assign any kind of clinical diagnosis for why Kim is the way she is, and I only know what Kim has disclosed about herself—which isn't much—but as an observant person with some sense, I can tell you that Kim just ain't right. She even tried lying on Lisa, although she denies it, and that lie could have cost Lisa her marriage. Thank God she and Ed were strong enough in the relationship not to believe that mess. At one point Kim let on she might have cancer and then said she didn't. Kim is not bald under that wig. She has hair but enjoys walking around looking trashy and thinking she's Barbie. Something is terribly off with her, and anyone who spends any significant amount of time around her kinda knows this.

So it makes sense that we're not friends now. Shoot, barely acquaintances. Kim and I continue to talk on an only-when-I-need-to-talk-to-you basis. But what you-all need to know is that I don't want to be Kim's friend.

As a matter of fact, I know now that I can't be anything more than an acquaintance to Kim.

She's simply too toxic for my ass.

And completely incapable of being a true friend.

THIS I KNOW FOR SURE

A word to the wise: Never trust a bitch to be a friend when you know she's sleeping with another woman's husband. Why? Because you know going into that "friendship" that she's not a trustworthy person, and she's an unstable creature.

Come on, now. You know we women have a code when it comes to other people's men: If he's wearing a ring, he's off-limits. Period. And any woman who breaks the Stay Away from Other Women's Men code is considered a home-wrecking tramp. She gets no love or respect from anybody, because we know her angle: She doesn't have any honor or decency or respect for you, yours, or herself. She's just out to do what makes her happy for the moment, and if she has to step on you, your children, your marriage, and your life to get it, then she will—especially if it means she'll benefit from it.

Now, if she's willing to do that to another woman, what makes you think she's not going to operate the same way in all of her relationships? See, chicks like that? The ones who break the Code? They have no loyalty, no allegiances. They're in it for self only—looking only for the score. And in their quest to win whatever the hell it is that they're trying to win—whether it be your man or your friends, your job or your connections—they will stomp anything in their path to get what they want. Their selfish ways, in other words, don't just rear their ugly heads when they're fooling around with someone else's husband. Those selfish ways show up in the boardroom, on the social scene, in their dealings with their family, and, in some cases, in friendships.

Just like she was willing to break the Code to sleep with another woman's man, she went above and beyond the call of duty to use me to get to Sheree. I wouldn't cosign her superficial ways, so she thought Sheree would—betraying our friendship in the process and proving to me that she's completely incapable of being loyal. I guess I should have been happy they found one another, so they could skip off into the sunset together, buying Prada and giving each other air kisses and shit.

But what you'll find with unstable creatures is that they will flip on your ass in a heartbeat. Sheree found out pretty quickly how nutty Kim can be when we attended Bravo's A-List Awards Show festivities together. Kim was walking around, acting the fool, spreading rumors and gossip and lies about us, her cast mates, to the housewives from the other shows.

Kim got *really* new on us that week. When she landed, she called us to let us know that she had her own personal driver and that she'd hired him to be her personal bodyguard and walk around with her, and that the hotel we were all supposed to stay in wasn't good enough so she was staying at the Peninsula. And when she finally did show up to the rehearsals, she acted like she didn't know who the hell Lisa, Sheree, and I were. She practically Super-Glued her ass to the other housewives, and then spent her entire time telling the other girls that she was the only one on the show with money, and that none of us liked her because we're broke and she's not, and that when she and Sheree got into it that Sheree punched her in the face. Of course, the other housewives came back and told us every word of what Kim was saying about us because they don't have any damn loyalty to her, and she's too stupid and deluded to recognize it. I swear, she's so high school it's pathetic. It's like she thought putting us down would make her look better in their eyes, like talking money to them would make them like her more. And besides, who the hell talks money like that to people you don't really know? And what makes her the authority on all of our bank accounts? Just because we don't waste money like she does doesn't mean we don't have it. It may just mean that we spend differently, that we have different priorities for our cash. I've always lived good and will continue.

Anyway, I don't think anybody was fooled by her antics. We all pretty much left the awards show convinced that Kim is probably the most unstable creature we know. And I don't do well with unstable creatures. For sure, she's got some serious self-esteem issues at best and, at worst, a serious need for prescription medication and a good talk with Jesus and his people. Because a woman who finds happiness in spending her days plotting and planning and scheming ways to take another woman's husband's money to drape herself in expensive trinkets definitely needs medication and Jesus—stat. I'm convinced that Kim is certifiably crazy.

And crazy people do not make good friends.

Ever.

I will never be friends with Kim's selfish, conniving, unloyal, snaky ass. A coworker? Yes. An acquaintance? For sure. But she taught me the very valuable lesson that some friendships aren't worth the effort, that it's okay to refuse the friendship of people who are crazy and deranged and willing to do anything to get what they want.

Chapter 12

WATCH THE GIRL WHO THROWS ROCKS
AND HIDES HER HANDS

My friend warned me about Sheree. "She's that girl who'll steal your girlfriend and use her until she's used all the way up," she told me when I called her to gab about the new girl she'd introduced me to a few days before. You know the type. She's your best friend—calls you on the phone and texts every second of the day, goes shopping with you, throws parties with you and goes with you to special events, too, gets close to your man and your kids and the dog, hell, everybody in your life. And then one day out of the blue, the chick you thought was your good friend meets one of your other good friends, and the next thing you know, they're off and running and painting the town purple and leaving you off the guest list like you don't matter, like you never existed.

I should have listened to my girl and heeded her warning.

But Sheree caught me off guard.

I met her about eight years ago when a mutual friend of ours was pregnant and a bunch of us were helping her celebrate her baby shower weekend. Friday was girlfriends' night out; there were six of us, and we went to a jazz bar, a cool spot to hang out in with a Friday night happy hour. They had a bad jazz band playing.

I was riding with one of my girlfriends who was picking up three or four other girls, Sheree included.

I'll never forget the first time I laid eyes on Sheree. She was the wife of Bob Whitfield, who played for the Atlanta Falcons at the time. They had a great big ol' house, a beautiful piece of property in one of the finest, most exclusive subdivisions in Georgia. The house gleamed like a new penny when you turned onto the street. I was sitting in the car just waiting to see who it was that lived in that bad boy.

And then Sheree walked out the front door looking like . . . the help. Real regular. She strolled up to my friend's Cadillac Escalade wearing a red velour sweat suit and with her hair curled all up tight against her head—old-school, hot-curlers-on-the-stove curly. So not fly. Not to me, anyway.

Anyway, we went to this cute little jazz spot downtown, had drinks and food and listened to some live music. It was a nice set, and by the end of the night, Sheree and I become friends, exchanging phone numbers and promising to keep in touch and get together for a little one-on-one friend time of our own.

Needless to say, we hit it off big-time. We weren't best friends, but we sure spent a lot of time together—traveled to Los Angeles together for All-Star Weekend, and to New York to support her while she trolled the fashion houses there, looking for hot clothes to bring back to her clothing boutique. We went to her house for Christmas and Thanksgiving, got our kids together for birthday celebrations.

Which is why I was shocked when Sheree said were just "associates." Let me be very clear: Our relationship was much bigger than that. An associate is someone you deal with only in times of necessity, a person with whom you have a working relationship that rarely, if ever, extends into personal business. Trust me when I tell you this: I was all up in Sheree's personal business because she invited me into it—not as an associate but as a trusted friend. Now, I wouldn't prove myself a good friend to anybody if I dished on all the intimate details Sheree shared with me. Those were personal, private moments she shared with me in confidence, and even though we're not friends anymore, I wouldn't feel right deep down in my gut if I aired out in these pages the secrets she trusted me with when we were girls. Lucky for her, I'm not *that* bitch.

But I need to make very clear that there were plenty of times that I was there for Sheree, plenty of times that I had her back while she was trying to make it through all the drama she had going on in her life. You just don't share all the I-need-to-keep-this-between-me-you-and-this-wall info with an "associate." The moments she shared with me—the crises I helped her through—included the level of detail you entrust to friends who will help you, sans judgment. That's the type of person I am; you can tell me anything and it won't matter to me how you got into that situation or how you're going to get yourself out of it—I don't give a shit.

So I beg to differ, Ms. Thing: We were much more than associates. Not BFF, but definitely cool enough to travel together and trust each other with some of the most intimate details of our lives.

DIRTY LOWDOWN

That is why I didn't see that Sheree left hook coming. Don't get me wrong, I knew that she was the type of chick who was trying to go to the next level and would stab you in the back to get there—the kind of woman who knows what she wants out of you and does what she needs to do to get what she wants out of you before she moves on to the next one.

But I thought because I was being a good friend to her, she would tell herself, "Nene is a good friend—be cool." That was my bad. I should have trusted my judgment enough to keep my guard up. But I didn't, and when people asked me for names of well-to-do African-American women who might be a good fit for their business ventures, I handed over Sheree's phone number and told them she might be someone they were looking for. Even crazier: After they talked to her and were struggling with whether to work with her—they thought she was boring as hell—I stood up for her. I admitted to them that she has a quiet side and isn't very outgoing, but I assured them that when she gets around us, we have a good time together, and insisted she would be a great addition. She'd called and questioned me about whether they said anything about her, but I hid the truth from her, like a good friend should in this instance. I didn't want to tell her they said she was boring. I just had her back, told them, "She's straight—put her on."

And so they did.

Now, you would think she would be grateful for that kind of hookup, would get a little act right in her if someone put her on a national platform with a paycheck and great exposure for the projects she was trying to get off the ground. But noooooooo, not Sheree. The moment she got in the public eye, she got *really* new. And our big fallout? It happened over a damn party. Can you believe it?

The way it went down was so simple and, well, stupid, but it was just the icing on the cake for the long line of wrong coming from Sheree's end. One particular night we were both getting ready for events around Atlanta. The two of us had been texting each other literally all day, talking about where we were going that night—except I was being really specific, and Sheree was being really vague with her details. Sneaky and secretive for no reason. She claimed it was a "private" affair and that it wasn't a big deal—"I'm putting on leggings and a shirt and I'm going to drop by."

I'm not really studying her party because I'm off to mine. But I let her know that I would call her when my party ended, and try to finish up the night at hers if she could get me in. Well, Sheree calls me all right, to tell me about all the stars that are walking into her hype party. So I ask her where she is so that I can meet her there, but she's still being really vague and won't tell me where she is. And somehow, we got "disconnected." After that, she stopped answering my phone calls and texts, the same ones she'd been sending and answering all day.

One would surmise from that mess that she didn't want me at the party, correct? Well, guess what? Nene had her own connects. It just so happens that the guy we were chilling with knew about the party going down at the Lucky Lounge and brought us right on in the front door, past the crowds and into the set, where Sean "P. Diddy" Combs was deejaying, and Usher, Kim Porter, the mother of Diddy's kids, and a bunch of other Atlanta heavyweights in the entertainment industry were partying.

Of course, I called and texted Sheree several times while I was there, but she didn't bother answering the phone. The next morning, she sent me a text asking me how my night went and I asked her in a text whether she enjoyed the party, because I personally thought it was "wack." She sent back a message saying, "How would you know?" I told her that I was there, which of course shocked the hell out of her, considering she was doing everything she could to hide from me.

Now, please don't get it twisted: I didn't get mad at her because she wouldn't invite me to some dumb party. I was tripping out because she was withholding information on where she was and deliberately being a bitch about it. She could have just as easily said, "Hey, the party is at the Lucky Lounge, but it's a private party and I can't get anybody in." That, I would have understood. But ignoring my phone calls and texts and acting like I wasn't worthy of being there in the same crowd as her? I decided right then and there that I didn't want to be friends with her. After everything I had done for her, she was playing judge and jury on whether I was good enough for her crowd?

Please.

I didn't tell her why—I just stopped calling her.

And she never called me again, either.

The next time I talked to Sheree was about a month later, when a bunch of us met at the Clubhouse at Lenox Mall. It was the first time Sheree and I were together before we started shooting, and of course we were gabbing about the show and how excited we were to get started with our new careers. Somehow we started talking about women we know in Atlanta, and when someone brought up Terry Ewing, the wife of a prominent car dealer in Atlanta, I said, "Oh, I know her—she's great."

Well, you would have thought I cursed Sheree's mama. I'd barely gotten the words out of my mouth before she snarled, "How would you know? You only met her once or twice."

Now why did she say that?

I. Went. Off.

I swear, I laid right into her in the Clubhouse. "Bitch, let me tell you something," I snapped back. "You're sitting at the table because of me. I went to bat for your Tasmanian devil ass, and you repay me by acting like I shouldn't be at a party? That shit rubbed me so fucking wrong after everything I've done for you, you dirty bitch!"

They had to drag me out of the Clubhouse.

It was that ugly.

And we never spoke again from that day forward, until we started working together.

THIS I KNOW FOR SURE

My aunt is from the country and she's full of country sayings. One of my favorites is this pearl: "Watch out for people who throw rocks and hide their hands." What she means is that smart people should watch out for people who stir up trouble, then stand back and watch the mayhem, claiming all the while that they didn't have anything to do with it.

Even worse, I let my bad experiences with her almost change who I am. No, I'm not talking about the public curse-out; you all know by now that I say what's on my mind and mean it when I say it. I admit I could have handled myself a little better that day in the Clubhouse—I do recognize that screaming in an upscale restaurant all seven of the words George Carlin once deemed unmentionable in public settings wasn't the best thing to do, and getting escorted out of a public venue is not exactly ladylike. Perhaps I could have expressed myself better, particularly in mixed company. Or just saved my cursing for a one-on-one with Sheree.

But really, the thing that I almost lost after fooling with Sheree was the thing that I think makes me special—my ability and willingness to be a good friend. Before Sheree and I got into it, I took great pride in simply being a good friend, being there when I was needed, helping in any way I could, giving of myself completely. I was that friend who would buy you a present just because it was a Monday, or cheer for you the loudest, even when *you* didn't envision yourself making it to the finish line, the friend who would drive you over to ol' what's-her-name's house to see if your man's car was parked outside. If the car was there, I'd be the first one to offer my shoulder to cry on. I thought nothing of lending folks cash when they needed it, getting them help if they required it, and keeping secrets.

Being a true friend is my specialty.

But Sheree almost changed that pearl in me, took me out of myself and made me fall into the trap that all too many women fall into when it comes to friendship. I'm convinced that women aren't very good at being friends; we can be some backstabbing, hurtful, dishonest, disloyal, evil people to other women, and for the stupidest reasons—"She didn't call me at four P.M. so now I hate her." "She went shopping with that chick I don't like, so now I hate her." "She wore blue to brunch and she knows how much I can't stand the color blue, so now I hate her." Too many of us are incapable of loving other female friends unconditionally, without judgment, ridicule, questioning, or hate. And forget about keeping a friend longer than a few weeks. How many girlfriends do you have who have been in your life for longer than a few months? A year? Since elementary school?

Well, I'd like to think that I go against the grain when it comes to friendship. When I decide I am going to be a woman's friend, it is important to me to be there for her, to be loyal. I have a big heart and have never backstabbed anyone to get to where I am today. But sometimes when people are trying to move up, they step on their friends. I've had experiences that have made it hard for me to trust other women. I now sometimes walk into a friendship guarded and go out of my way to avoid giving freely of myself.

Avoid being me.

But I now know that I can't let a bitch change who I am. I'm surrounded by women friends who love me, trust me, and are true to me. Those are the women I shower with love and friendship, because they deserve it. I'm more guarded now when it comes to making new friends, that's for sure. Part of this is because of the celebrity, but a large chunk of my guardedness comes from my wanting to make sure that I never encounter another fake friend. I've decided not to let so many women in so easily. The truth is what happened with Sheree hurt me. To think you are cool with someone and to go out of your way to be helpful and do nice things for them, only to have them turn around and pretend the friendship never existed was like getting slapped in the face. It was painful.

Now, Sheree and I have since had our "Come to Jesus" moment, and she's apologized to me for some of the things she said and did during our tumultuous relationship, I apologized for anything I'd done wrong to her and she even said she appreciated the way that Gregg and I helped her through some of her more trying times. I accepted her apology, and we've both agreed to move on. I never thought these words would come out my mouth, but Sheree does have a cool side to her and I've seen her make some changes to her attitude. She is definitely easier to be around and I'm genuinely glad to see her move on with her life and find a happier her. We definitely had a beef with each other, but I'm glad we found a way to respect each other for who we are. She's definitely easier to be around and seems to be that cool Sheree I used to kick it with. I even think I noticed a slight change in her personality. I think she's changing because you can be so mean and hateful for only so long. God will humble you. Since her divorce, she's now living in a much more modest home than the one she shared with her ex-husband. I'm guessing she had to marinate on that. She'd been spending like budgets weren't a thing and acting like a coldhearted bitch every chance she got. I know she, and a lot of other people, think the word "bitch" is a derogatory term and I can agree with that, but I'm just calling it like I saw it then and see it today. Sheree is a bitch. It's a part of her.

People say I'm hood and ghetto, and I'll take that because I do know how to get hood. I didn't grow up in any financially depressed household, and though my aunt and uncle weren't rich, we sure didn't want for anything, so I can't and won't claim the ghetto. But I do have some ghetto tendencies. I know how to hold a meeting down and be professional, but if I'm riding in the car and I happen to be eating some chicken, I might just toss the bone out the window. You might see me in a store with a long line of customers behind me, getting loud with the manager when the girl on the register isn't giving me what I need. You might catch me getting a little loud and wrong while I'm drinking from a straw—I tend to slurp a little bit. Even though I don't necessarily like the term or care for people to label me as such, yes ma'am, I can get hood. Just like Sheree can be a bitch. She reminds me of that girl from the hood who just decided to become a diva and be foul to folks for no other reason than that she can. It is what it is.

I don't think the old Sheree is totally gone. She's still *that* girl. But she is trying to make changes and I can believe that. I saw the better Sheree come out when we attended the A-List Awards. It's going to take me a minute to let other women in, too. But you best believe, the ones who get close—who earn my loyalty—have my heart.

Friends for life.

Chapter 13

BEING A PART OF THE IN CROWD IS
CUTTHROAT—BUT YOU SHOULD KNOW
THAT "FOOL" IS *NOT* SPELLED N.E.N.E.

There isn't a drug out there that can get you higher than celebrity. Walking on the red carpet, having the paparazzi yell out your name and tell you to look this way and that way, walking right up to the front of the longest lines and having people escort you into the VIP room just because they know your name and face, collecting big-time paychecks just for showing up to the party—all of this is, quite simply, addictive. What I can't stand, though, is the attention you get from your so-called friends. People who couldn't be bothered with me before the show are blowing up my phone nowadays, inviting me to lunch, grabbing my hand at the parties, introducing me to this one and that one, sending drinks over to my table and FedEx'ing gifts to the house. Honey, these people are a trip! Especially since I know, and they know too, that they weren't paying my ass any kind of mind before *The Real Housewives of Atlanta* hit.

I live in a country club community in a pricey suburb of Atlanta, where the security guards check every car that even thinks about turning in the direction of the huge iron gates separating the average home from the million-dollar homes of me and my neighbors. And the people who live here? Let's just say they've got a little extra pep in their step because they feel like they've "made it." Anyone they deem unacceptable to their exclusive, well-to-do circles gets soundly ignored. And I've been no exception. The same women who drive their Benzes and BMWs and Range Rovers past my house to get to their driveways, who bump into me in the bread aisle at the grocery store, whose children play with my children during recess at the local school, who get their pedicures in the next chair over from me at the nail salon, would just as soon cut their tongues clean out of their mouths than loosen their lips to speak to me before I was on TV. Now that I've got a show they're watching, those same women are running up to me while I'm out and about around town, talking about, "Oh, my God! You're on the show! You should come play tennis with us! I'll bring a basket to the house! Let's get together!"

Yeah, uh-huh. But last week, those same heiffas were giving me the side eye because I wouldn't join in on the conversation about the new Gucci bag they saw in some magazine.

Right. And no one was more obvious about this than an acquaintance of mine, whom I'll call "Miss C." Now, Miss C is the mother of a prominent Atlanta celebrity; we live near each other, and we've rolled in the same circles for the longest. When we'd run into each other while we were out and about town, she'd always take the time to make conversation; I thought she was cool people. But don't let us be somewhere and she's got her groupies in tow. Then all of a sudden, the cat's got her tongue and she can't open her damn mouth. They'll be over there posted up in the corner, comparing baubles and scheming on which rich guy they're going to try to kick it with, and whispering about people who dare darken their doorway in outfits and shoes they deem insufficiently expensive or impressive. I mean, these are some catty bitches. And Miss C? She's the Queen Bee—would be standing right there in the middle of all of them, holding court and acting like every tooth in her mouth would fall right out of her head if she opened her damn mouth to say hello to somebody.

Here's what she didn't know, though, and probably won't until she reads this sentence right here: I don't care if she and her friends speak to me or not because I could give a rat's ass about what she or they have to say. It's not like she's talking about anything anyway. Miss C is the first one to brag about all of her designer clothes and her luxurious trips and the kinds of cars she's pushing—you know, making sure anyone within the sound of her voice feels adequately inadequate. "Ooh, girl, you should see this new purse I just picked up at Louis—it's fabulous and I know nobody else has it," she'd purr before you could get within earshot. "Ooh, that cute little man I've been talking to is taking me to Europe—ta ta!" And with every breath she'd take, Miss C would be staring you down with that X-ray vision of hers, calculating how much you paid for your shoes and your dress and your bag and your lip gloss and your last pedicure, manicure, and hairstyle appointments, and then giving you the half-hearted, "Oh, those are, um, cute shoes, girl." The wrinkled nose and the narrowed eyes were a dead giveaway that her compliment was meant as a backhanded slap, that she's trying to make you look like a fool.

Oh, she would burn me up with that mess. Be clear: I'm not jealous of her ass by any stretch. I just can't stand it when evil women like her lord their "things" over others and treat people who aren't dripping in diamonds and gold or, in my case, don't *want* to, like we're beneath her and her superficial friends. I mean, come on, now: This chick, and plenty more well-to-do women like her, acts like cute shoes are going to cure cancer, like if they were laid up in a hospital bed dying, a team of doctors could roll a sparkling new Gucci bag in on a crash cart and use it to revive their asses. Right.

Don't get it twisted: I like nice stuff. Like I said earlier, I choose not to spend *all* of my hard-earned money on clothes and handbags and shoes and things. In fact, I think you're a good shopper if you can find cute things anywhere, not just in expensive, name-brand boutiques. In fact, a girl who can go into T.J. Maxx and come out with a fly outfit without having seen it in a magazine or on some celebrity has more style, in my book, than the woman who keeps going back to the same three stores, picking up dresses and shirts and purses and things just because of what the tag says. Plus, it's more fun to shop in the bargain stores—the treasure is in the find.

Of course, I can't shop in stores like T.J. Maxx anymore, or the next thing you know, I'll turn on the 11 o'clock news and the lead story will be, "Our cameras caught Nene Leakes shopping in T.J. Maxx—the bitch is broke." Now I have to sneak in that store when it's first open, or when it's about to close, or I have to send somebody in there for me, which takes away from the whole experience because I want to look for myself. That's just the hand you're dealt when you're in the spotlight. But it doesn't mean that when I'm around women who live like I live, have what I have, and enjoy the spotlight like I do, all we can talk about is how much money we're spending on bullshit. What about your kids? How are they doing in school? How's your marriage going? Does your husband still love you? Are you doing anything interesting to better yourself? What's *really* good with you?

MY TV HUSBAND

All that superficial mess? Talk it while you're walking. I'd much rather spend time with people like Dwight. People think we've known each other for years, but really Dwight and I didn't start kicking it until about two years ago. I knew about him going on twenty years now. When I came to Atlanta for college, he owned the Purple Door, a superpopular salon over in Buckhead. His salon was pricey, but the stylists in there did some good work. I'd never sat as a client in his chair, though, and we'd known each other only in passing until a mutual friend asked me to meet up with her at Dwight's salon, where she was getting her hair done. From the moment we met, we just connected, and it wasn't long before we were exchanging phone calls and having lunch together.

What I love about Dwight is that he's a confident, intelligent, down-to-earth diva—the kind of man who enjoys dressing nicely and eating on the good china and using the good silverware and wiping his mouth with a cloth napkin and wearing eyelashes and getting his French pedicures, but who would never pass judgment on you if that wasn't *your* way. People, me included, want to be around him not only because he's a fun guy who cares about nurturing friendships, but also because he's very involved in fund-raising for AIDS awareness and is intimately involved in fighting for gay rights, which to me means he cares about more than just the superficial crap some celebrities train on. I also love that Dwight is real and knows what he wants; he reminds me of, well, me. I think that's why Dwight keeps asking me to have his baby! I just say, "No, honey, I cannot have a baby with you, but we can figure out a way for you to have one with somebody else, how about that? Because there will *not* be a Nene and Dwight baby, hear?"

Of course, then he tells me that I might be a lesbian.

"Chile, please! I'm not a lesbian, Dwight," I say. "I like men, specifically, my husband, Gregg."

"Well, how do know? Have you ever slept with a woman?"

"No, Dwight," I say, shaking my head. "I've never slept with a woman."

"You need to sleep with a woman to find out if you're a

lesbian, or you'll never know for sure." He laughs. "You only live once. You should try it."

"We're just going to stick to what we do around here, thank you," I say, laughing just as easily.

We could go on like that for hours—our chemistry is ridiculous. Whenever we get together, it's on—because he's a diva and I'm a diva, but we're not ugly to people, at least not on purpose. Dwight is the sweet diva who brings out the realness— you don't get that drama from him. He'll compliment something on you that he likes, whether you're beautiful or you're not, and he'll ask you about your day and be genuinely interested in listening to what you have to say. Now, after you warm up, he might say, "Honey, those shoes now . . ." but he won't be fake about it, and he certainly won't say it just to see how much he can hurt you. He's not messy or gossipy like that.

And neither am I.

So though he's not my kind of baby daddy, he's definitely my kind of friend—someone who's real, isn't trying to use me to get ahead, and appreciates me for me.

In the ever-fake entertainment industry, he's a rare jewel, indeed.

THIS I KNOW FOR SURE

I like the in crowd. I've always been in it, from the time I was in high school and we were carving ourselves into little cliques. I wasn't always the prettiest girl in the mix, but I was tall and confident, which made me sexy and popular. The problem with popular, though, is that it's cutthroat, and every night you have to count how many knives have been stuck in your back from all the backstabbing. The wounds can cut deep—if you let them. You have to be vigilant about what you say, how you say it, and whom you say it to—and especially the company you keep. And you have to stay true to who you are.

If you're not a strong person, being a celebrity can change who you are with a quickness. When the show hit and people were starting to recognize me, I did start mixing it up. I started talking proper and changing the tone and volume of my voice, and acting like someone other than Nene. All of that came to a screeching halt, though, when I really listened to myself. I sounded ridiculous. I've lived almost my entire life in Georgia, and I was raised in Nena Thomas's house, which means I have a little bit of a country accent, and I got a lot of country sayings I picked up along the way. And I've been loud and tell it like it is from the day I entered this world, and I cannot—simply will not—change that for anybody. I don't have to, and I don't want to, because I like being me exactly the way I am. The people who can't get with that—who look down on me like I'm beneath them—can step to the left, because this is me, baby. I've always been uncomfortable with being fake; it just works better for me when I'm being Nene.

Do understand that the way I get on the phone and talk to my girls is not the way I go into a business meeting. I'm not about to walk in that boardroom cursing or gossiping about people or being ridiculously loud, because that's not business-like, period. I can most certainly switch gears for certain situations, especially when I'm about to make deals. I'm a professional. But I've learned that I can still be myself and professional all at the same time. If I get invited into the boardroom to discuss one of my projects, and I'm acting stuck up and phony like you're beneath me and I'm doing you a favor by sitting at your table, then whoever is trying to do business with the real Nene Leakes is going to be disappointed, isn't she? Because my image—my persona—would be quite different from what most people have come to expect from me. I put people at ease, I tell it like I see it, and I'm funny—a can't-lose combination.

I've learned to look for those traits when I decide whether I'm going to let you in or not—to help me figure out if you're for real, or if you're just a poser trying to use me to get something for yourself. I was sucked into that madness with Sheree and Kim, but I'm not about to have that happen again. I know now that if you were a bitch before you had money or fame, you'll be a bigger bitch when you get a little cash and a name.

That's why Miss C and her little groupies won't get anything but the flat hand from me. Oh, trust: She thinks she's slick. After months of acting like she didn't know me any better than the postman, Miss C finally picked up the phone and called me. And wouldn't you know it, that phone call came literally within days of the debut episode of the show. She was kissing my ass all kinds of different ways—calling my cell phone and the house, too, inviting me to her place for drinks. I'd just blow her off—I'd either let her calls go to voice mail, or cut the conversation real short so that she wouldn't ever get the impression that I really cared about what she had to say. When she invited me to dinner a few days after the casting announcement for season 2 went out, I finally took her up on her offer. I giggled to myself just anticipating how long it would take her to get around to asking me if I could recommend her as another house-wife. We didn't get through the appetizers good before she was making her pitch.

"I think I would be just perfect for it, don't you?" she asked.

I smiled and nodded on the outside, but on the inside, I was laughing and throwing up a little in my mouth and yelling, "Aren't you the same bitch that thought I was beneath you? And now you need *my* help to get what you want? Puh-leeze!"

"Sure," I said enthusiastically. "I'll refer you."

And I finished up my dinner and my drinks, air-kissed her good-bye, and promptly told myself that I would pluck the nails off my toes one by one before I'd recommend her to be on a TV show with me. It simply was not going to happen, not if I had anything to do with it.

When she didn't hear back from me, though, Miss C called Lisa looking for an in. I told Lisa to put the kibosh on that shit, too. She wasn't about to get on national TV and disrespect my ass—I've had enough of that already.

See, all kinds of shady, bougie women who acted like I was beneath them are now treating me like I'm the toast of the town, like they just have to have me over for dinner and drinks and bonding because they like me so much. I know the deal, though: They just want in on *The Real Housewives of Atlanta*, and now, the same women who thought I wasn't good enough for them last month are treating me like their "must-have" accessory. I got their numbers, though. The one thing Nene's not going to do is be used.

So while Miss C is over there spinning her wheels trying to figure out how to get on the show, I'll be kicking it with real chicks who aren't superficial, like my new friend, Melissa. Her husband is a player in the real estate game, and the two of them moved into the neighborhood from what she says was a "modest" house. And wouldn't you know it: None of the women who live here, the wives of surgeons and lawyers and real estate moguls and major players in Fortune 500 companies, will talk to her. "I didn't grow up with all of this," she confided once when were kicking it at a restaurant not too long ago. "And I certainly don't have any Gucci, Prada, Dolce, or all those fancy clothes the women around here seem to always talk about. I think that's why they don't like me."

She was warning me that the women who lived in our neighborhood appear nice at first, but are gossipy and don't think you're on their level if you don't stay at home and be nosy. That, she said, is why they don't talk to her. Your husband has to be somebody or *you* have to be somebody in order for them to pay attention to you. You can't be an average girl.

I already knew how those women were. But around me, you can be you. In fact, I'll take an "average" girl over a fake, rich girl any day, because the rich, fake girl is out for herself and looking to hurt somebody to get what she wants, and would run over my dead, prone body if she had to in order to get it. I'm no fool. I'll take Melissa any day of the week. I'm more comfortable around people like her, people a little more real about it. I figure that if you're cool and down-to-earth, you're going to stay that way. And there'll be less of a chance that you'll try to play me out.

Chapter 14

ME, MYSELF, AND I IS ALL I GOT IN THE END

I knew growing up that I could truly do anything, that I could be anything I wanted to be. But knowing it and being it are two whole different things, especially if someone else is blinding you with money and fancy clothes and nice cars and the celebrity that comes from having and flashing cash. For sure, I had big dreams of being a star before I met Gregg. I wasn't sure how I was going to be one, but I knew I had it in me, and all I needed was a shot. Still, I got sidetracked trying to make enough quick money to be sure my baby boy was fed and had a roof over his head. I put my dreams of being an actress aside again when I married Gregg, a businessman who owned several cellular phone companies and had quite a bit of success in the real estate industry. When we got together, I was coming into motherhood and really starting to understand that stripping wasn't going to get it anymore. Bryson was about to be in the first grade, and I needed him to start school with me not dancing in the club. And here was this beautiful man, whom I loved and who loved me back, telling me that I didn't have to dance anymore, that he would take good care of my son and me. Like a *real* man should, and definitely not like my ex, who'd proved time and again with his lack of support—financially, emotionally, and physically—that he had no intention of doing right by me. Gregg knew what to do. He had money *and* he knew how to be a good father and a good husband. Marrying him was a no-brainer. He was everything I'd ever hoped to find in a husband, for sure, everything my aunt had told me I should look for in the guy I'd choose to be the head of my family.

See, my aunt is old school, the kind of woman who firmly believes that it's a man's duty to provide for his family. Oh, a woman can work—Lord knows my aunt certainly did the whole time we were coming up and she was raising my brother and me. But she had some pearls of wisdom and didn't have a problem sharing them, particularly the ones she picked up while working as a cook at a fraternity house in Athens. She got an up-close-and-personal view of those nutty college kids, and one of the takeaways she kept drilling into me was how important it was for me not only to get married, but to marry a man who was successful—like the girls who were going to school up there in Athens. "Those girls marry up, Nene," she'd told me on more than a few occasions. "Their parents come up to the school and they say, 'Oh, my daughter's dating an attorney' and 'My daughter's dating a doctor.' They know what they're doing. They're setting themselves up so they don't have to worry about working. Those men are going to take care of them, honey. That's what you need to do, too. Don't go out there and marry no broke man who can't do anything for you, hear?"

I respect my aunt's opinion, and I learned a lot from her too—took what she had to say about men to heart, especially the "marry up" part. You couldn't be broke and be with Nene, no, ma'am. You could be hot and sexy and everything and sparks could be flying like a rocket off a launchpad at Cape Canaveral and whatnot, but the moment a boy told me he didn't have any money and his conversation was lame, all that rocket love shit went right out the window. I could not, would not, and will not ever sleep with someone with no cash in the bank and no good conversation—period. I can't do it. But a guy who wasn't the best looking in the world and not as sexy could always get some play if he had something going for himself and he had good conversation and he was attracted to me. The success would take his ass up a notch or two.

That's not to say I'm some gold digger, because I'm not. A true gold digger in my book goes after only one type of guy and depends on him to be her beginning, middle, and end. Her only ambition in life is to marry an athlete, singer, or actor with big-time money, so that she can take her credit cards and cash and go shopping, and then be presented around town as the "significant other," when she knows good and well she's nothing more than arm candy for the guy with the gold. It's only a step above groupie, really, especially if you date only one specific type of guy.

I, however, am not a gold digger. Sure, I can appreciate the "marry up" part and I've always required the men I go with to have more than me, be able and willing to provide for me and my family, and be into me completely before I'd give them even a half a look. But I've never wanted to be the woman who sat around spending her man's money. No, I wanted to live comfortably while I pursued my passions, and having a man with money was always essential for my climb to the top.

IN CONTROL

It didn't start out this way when I first got with Gregg, though—I'll be truthful about that. After we got married and we had our son Brentt together, I became a stay-at-home mom who got really comfortable letting her husband handle all of the affairs. I wanted for nothing and did little; he paid every bill, planned every vacation, knew how to get the cable and lights and heat turned on whenever we moved, and generally took charge of most every aspect of our life, with little to no help from me. If we were going on vacation, I'd give the okay for the destination, and then he'd handle everything else—where we'd stay, how we'd get there, and how we'd get back home. If we were moving, I'd give the okay on the house, and then he'd handle all the rest—the moving, getting the business part straight, all of that. And guess what? I didn't care that he had control over the logistics. It was nice to be able to do what I wanted to do and raise my sons the way I wanted to raise them all without worrying where the next dime would come from.

Nice, that is, until I realized that I had no control.

I started itching for my own independence, wanting to stop depending on my man for every little thing. Before I got with Gregg, I was always working. When I was with my ex, I was out modeling, and after I got out of my relationship with him, I was dancing. I'd always had my own money, never had to ask anyone for any kind of help. And I lost that hunger when I got with a man who was financially stable and made it possible for me to stay home and raise our son until he was old enough to go to school on his own. At the end of the day, Gregg owned the house I lived in; he was the one paying for the food on our table and my visits to the hair salon and the nail salon. Hell, I couldn't buy a box of sanitary products without withdrawing money from the family bank account full of *his* money. And if he had that kind of rein over the bank account, it meant that he had that kind of rein over me.

I couldn't stand this. It's certainly nice to want for nothing, but I have dreams and ambitions, and I didn't like putting them on hold—not even for the love of my life. Instead, I wanted to be that woman who made her man's cash work for her. Tracey Edmonds, Kenneth "Babyface" Edmonds's ex-wife, figured it out. She wasn't content to sit around spending her singer/songwriter husband's millions. She took his money and started her own film production firm that had a string of successful projects in Hollywood and on television, including, most famously, the superpopular film *Soul Food.* Now, even though they're not together anymore, Tracey is still doing her thing as the head of Edmonds Entertainment. She knew what to do with Babyface's cash, for sure.

Kimora Lee Simmons knew what to do with her ex's

bank account, too. The two of them built a fashion empire that extended into Kimora founding her own brand—Baby Phat. She designs and distributes women's clothes, children's clothes, shoes, handbags, perfume, jewelry—has her own television reality show, too, chronicling how she turned her ex's cash into her own fame and fortune. She saw the vision and worked it like no other, honey.

Kimora is my inspiration. It was she who showed me the vision—that the hustle and the independence are ultimately much more empowering than running around the malls spending someone else's money and trying to maintain all of that superficial shit your man fell in love with so that he won't leave your ass for the next prettier, younger, hotter chick. I saw the vision, and I did what I needed to do to position myself for greatness. That meant that I had to get out there, try out for roles, hit pilot season out in Los Angeles, make connections in the film and television industry, and be ready with an armful of fresh ideas that would stretch my fifteen minutes of TV fame.

And now I'm one of the hottest—if not *the* hottest— stars on Bravo. Be clear: We're not doing these shows for free. We get paid to work for Bravo, and those checks go toward paying bills, hiring attorneys, negotiating contracts, and making valuable connections in the industry that could turn into lucrative deals later on down the line. Indeed, at the end of the first season of *Real Housewives*, I had four more deals in the works, including another season of the show, this book deal, and a line of handbags. And the Nene gravy train doesn't stop there— trust. *The Real Housewives of Atlanta* provides a great platform for a bunch of other things, including endorsements, appearance fees, speaking engagements, and the like. Those are big contracts, offered by people with big money, money that allows me to live the life I am accustomed to living, without feeling indebted to a man.

Even if he's the man I love.

I take great pride in that.

THIS I KNOW FOR SURE

After all of these years raising my kids and being a good wife and taking great care of our home, I'm the breadwinner now—and the star I always knew I could be. Now I can stand on my own two feet and make my own decisions about my life, my career. And it feels good! When I get phone calls from producers and publicists, celebrities and entrepreneurs asking me—me!—to go on their shows and consider their projects, I get tickled just knowing that people finally recognize that I truly can do anything. Sometimes, it does feel like I'm starting over, like my life has just begun. Before *The Real Housewives of Atlanta* first hit the air, I'd been a housewife for eleven years and spent every minute of that time letting my husband take care of me. He did a fine job of it, too; his hard work made life for our kids and me extremely comfortable—we wanted for nothing. Gregg made sure of that.

But now I'm in control of our financial destiny, and that feels damn good. Not just because the money is good, but because my family, and especially I, get to depend on *me* for a change. When I get my hair done, I'm paying with money I earned. When I have friends over for a dinner party and I want to serve the finest food and drinks money can buy, those expensive steaks and wines are courtesy of moi. If I want a new car, I can go on ahead and get it, without guilt. I know the cash is there because I put it there.

I'll tell you, too, that sometimes it feels like I'm starting over, like my life has just begun. I know for sure now that I *can* be successful without my husband. This is not taking away from anything he's done for me—for our family—over the past decade-plus. I appreciate the man he is, and how he stepped up to the plate and went to bat for me and mine, no questions asked, from the moment he met me. My friends would always say, "I don't know what you're complaining about. Gregg is a helluva man and takes good care of you," and I won't disagree with that statement. It is true. But every woman should have the chance to see what it feels like to run things. It's the most powerful, wonderful feeling ever, I promise you.

And now that I have true independence, I want to help other women see that they, too, have the power to focus on their goals and bring their dreams to fruition. I want to do an Independent Woman tour to school some of these young women, hip them to some *real* game. Because all too often these days, it's those young women who get caught up on what a guy has and how much of it they can get, rather than focusing on what they can get for themselves. I want to let them know that they can date rich men, but that they should take a page from Tracey Edmonds and Kimora Lee Simmons and Nene Leakes, too, and have their own thing going, so that they can experience the wonderful feeling you get when you know you've got control, power, and, most important, freedom. At the end of the day, we all deserve freedom, don't we? And you simply can't have that if you're too busy depending on someone else to get you what you need and want.

I should have learned that lesson while I was with my ex. I had nowhere to go and felt like I was stuck with him, not only because we had a baby together but also because his mother used to let me stay with them when I had nowhere else to go. Of course, staying there gave him power over me because he got to control whether I got to lay my head down in their house at night, and what my son and I would be eating for dinner, and whether we would be going out or staying in, and whether I would be able to go to sleep at night without having been beaten. Being with him was the antithesis of power, the antithesis of freedom.

While my relationship with Gregg was, of course, much more evolved, at the end of the day I still didn't have the freedom I needed to be Nene the star. But now I have my own thing going on. And as a reward to him for taking care of me and supporting me and my dreams for so long, now I would love to turn the tables and take care of him. Gregg jokes all the time that now that I'm bringing home the bacon, he's going to retire and start shopping for a new set of golf clubs so that he can be a man of leisure.

I'm not mad at him for that.

He deserves to be happy, to relax after all of these years of taking such good care of me and mine. And if I can have a hand in making that happen, then dammit, I'm going to make it happen.

And then I'll relish in my newfound independence, because it just feels so damn good.

There's much more to come for Nene Leakes—I'm just getting started. This may be the final chapter of my book, but my story isn't over.

Not by a stretch.

Because Nene's not going anywhere.

Chapter 15

TWENTY QUICK WAYS I'VE LEARNED TO AVOID MISTAKES AND WORK ON ME

Of course, I've got work to do—I'm not perfect. Who is? I've made it through a lot of storms in my life, but today I'm getting mine, feeling fantastic, and living the life—and I know that it's only going to get better. I'm *so* happy being me! Here, I'm sharing with you some of the things I've done and continue to do to help me move forward from the challenges I've faced, with the hopes that it can inspire you to move past the bull and keep it moving toward a better you.

I'm building a better life with my kids by . . .

1. **Sharing my mistakes with them.** I've made a lot of them, that's for sure. I'm not ashamed of most of the things I did in my past that others might find questionable, but I certainly am glad that I went through them because they made me the person I am today—brought me to this very moment. But as a mom, I want to make sure that I have a hand in helping my kids avoid those pitfalls as best I can, and I'm doing that by letting them know about all of my mess. I figure if they can hear firsthand how much I struggled because I didn't have someone telling me about even the simplest things, like how to establish credit and how to pay bills on time and how important it is to stick with your education, and pick the people you date well, then they'll be less likely to make the same mistakes I made. I know they have to live their lives, and that mistakes are going to happen—that's the nature of kids. But my job as a parent is to help them avoid as many of them as I humanly can. I can't help but to think that telling them about my mess will help them stay out of their own.

2. **Being an equal partner with my husband.** Gregg calls it the good cop/bad cop way of parenting. I call it balance. I admit that I'm a little less strict with the boys—call me a softie! But I need them to know that they are loved, and I don't want to always be the one hollering and screaming at them. So I'm the hugger in the relationship, and Gregg is much more the disciplinarian and the one who steps up to teach them about what it takes to be a good man. This way, both of us are participating in their upbringing, and they

can use our relationship as an example of what they should be looking for in their own relationships, especially as they get ready to have families of their own. I'm hoping that they can see the beauty of what Gregg and I have created.

3. **Letting Gregg be a daddy to Bryson.** My son's father hasn't been in his life in any meaningful way. Gregg, however, has been in my son's life way longer than he's been out of it. Indeed, Gregg was there when I registered Bryson for his first day in first grade. And he loves Brice like his blood runs through his veins, like a real father loves his own child. I've always appreciated this about Gregg, because it could have been much easier for him to run in the other direction than to help raise a child who's not his own. Still, he stepped up to the plate, and I made sure to stay out of his way while he was being a parent to my child. There are some women who can't quite handle this, maybe because they're used to being the sole parent to their kids, or because they want to force a relationship between their children and the biological dads. I understand why a woman would try those approaches, but I found that opening the door to let Gregg love my son as his own helped mold my child into a fine young man and made the blending of our families that much easier.

4. **Letting my boys be who they want to be.** Like any mother, I have some pretty firm ideas of what I want my sons to be in life and how they can achieve success. What mother doesn't want that for her child? But while I might want my kids to go to college and become lawyers and marry and have babies and live fabulously, they may not necessarily want that for themselves. I realize that I can't force them to live the life I want them to live. I have to give them my ad-

vice, then step back and let them live the lives they choose. It was difficult for me to accept that Brice didn't attend college and decided to pursue a career as a nightclub/events promoter, but he's a young man now with the right to make his own decisions. The best I can do for him is to give him my advice without demanding he take it, and, above all else, be there for him—provide that safety net in the event that he falls. It's the only way he's going to find his way.

5. **Not overdoing it and giving my kids everything they want.** My kids are spoiled. I'll cop to that. But they know, too, the importance of a dollar and how hard it is to earn one, and why it's important to be smart about spending it. These boys have to work for what they get. You want a new video game? Bring home the grades to prove that you deserve it. Otherwise, get your butt in the room and study so you can earn the right to have Mommy give you nice things. Period.

6. **Trying not to smother them.** This one I struggle with the most. It's not easy for a mother to let go of her children, to unleash them into a cold, harsh, unforgiving world. But they've got to learn from their mistakes, just like I did mine. I try to remind them best I can that I hold tight to them because they are flesh of my flesh and blood of my blood, and I love them and want the best for them. But I also try to remind myself that they've got to find their way, and holding on to them so tightly could stifle their ability to be. I get it. I'm trying.

I'm trying to be a better friend by . . .

7. **Not trying to fix everybody.** I think I'm a damn good friend—I go hard for my girls. But I do recognize that they can't be me any more than I can be them. And it's unfair for me to try to force them to think like me and do like me and move like me. Not everyone has that ability, and everyone has the right to be who she is. I have a big heart, so when my friends are suffering or going through some things, my first inclination is to step in and see how we can fix it, even if my friend isn't ready for it to be fixed just yet, or fixed the way I would like to see it fixed. Change is a process, and sometimes it moves slowly. I'm trying my best to respect that.

8. **Being more forgiving.** This is not an easy thing to do. When someone burns you, you remember only the burn, not all of the other things that may have made you feel good before the burning commenced. I have to constantly remind myself that people aren't perfect, and that they're going to make mistakes, and sometimes, people they really care about may get hurt in the process. Now, some bitches might not give a damn who gets hurt by their shenanigans, and those women don't deserve my forgiveness. But the ones who are willing to work with me to get over the hump get my attention. And with a little work, they might also get my friendship back. This isn't easy for me. But I'm working on it.

9. **Taking the time to be a real friend.** The schedule is busy. I'm a mom and a wife, I have a TV show, and I'm an entrepreneur. Time is limited. But that's no excuse for not being

there when my friends need me. The ones who know how hectic my schedule is understand that I can't hang with them like I used to, but I've made a point of letting them know—and showing them through my actions—that I'm there when it counts, whether it is a simple phone call to check up on them and see how they're hanging in, or helping them work through whatever issues they have by giving them sound advice and the resources to make it through.

10. **Not downplaying my mistakes.** I've been wrong many times. And I've done things to some friends that may not have been nice. These days, I'm good at apologizing for my mistakes and really thinking about why they may have happened so that we don't have to face it again. I've made a point of apologizing to people and thinking about how I could have acted better in situations with them. Now, that doesn't mean I'm ever going to be everybody's friend again; some of them don't deserve it. But I learned a valuable lesson in those situations, and I'll be sure to remember if and when I ever make a mistake in a friendship that's worth keeping.

11. **Spending more time listening.** Sometimes, it's just better to keep your mouth shut. I know the value of this, though I don't always practice it. I do know, though, that when people you care about are able to work through their issues without you passing judgment and spoon-feeding them the prescription, they're more likely to understand why they're in the predicament they're in, and especially how they can get out of it. A true friend listens and offers support, sans judgment. I'm trying that one out for size, too.

I'm trying to build a stronger marriage
with my husband by . . .

12. **Spending quality time with him.** This isn't easy, particularly in the business I'm in. People intrude on our lives when we're just trying to have time to ourselves. We can't have a dinner together or a cocktail or go to a movie without it being a huge production and fans inserting themselves into our personal space. This annoys Gregg to no end, particularly because he's not in the business. To help stave off the hard feelings, we try to find ways to get away together, even if it's just to sit in the house and watch a show, or sneak out of town to a quiet hotel where we can escape from the constant pull on our lives.

13. **Supporting his goals.** My husband is a businessman, always has been. And just like any true businessman, he's constantly thinking of ways to reinvent himself and discover new projects and goals to tackle. Now that I'm a businesswoman, I can understand this and appreciate it. So when he discovers yet another thing that he can get into, he gets my total support.

14. **Listening more.** I'm an opinionated woman and it's easy for me to talk all the way over you to get my point across. While I'm talking, I may not be listening to what he has to say—I admit that. But I do know that my husband is a wise man and has strong opinions and good observations about situations, and it's useful to let him have his say. I'm trying to use my listening ears, I promise you that.

15. **Letting him look.** Let me tell you this: Looking ain't never

hurt nobody, so long as it's done in a respectful manner. He's not going to be making catcalls after anybody and acting the fool if he sees someone cute, but my man has eyes and it's okay for him to appreciate beauty. Trust: Gregg knows not to touch, and he also knows to respond to women who try to put it on him, with, "Are you kidding me? Step back. I'm married to Nene." Yup.

16. **Trying not to hold on to him too hard.** Like every couple, Gregg and I have our ups and downs, and there are times when his stubbornness or my ambition or our mutual exhaustion gets in the way of our progress. I think we're both clear that if we're not happy, we'll do what we can to make it work. But if we just can't do it anymore, we both know that we've had a good run and that hanging on for the sake of hanging on wouldn't be healthy for either of us. This is a mature way of looking at relationships. It's not easy. But it is mature.

17. **Asking for help.** A man likes to feel appreciated—I do realize this. There's just a large part of me that's happy to be an independent woman again. I spent a lifetime fighting and scratching and surviving for myself and my first son, and then I spent another chunk of my life depending on my husband while I took care of our kids and our home. These days, I'm so happy to be able to make decisions for myself and have what I'm doing positively impact our finances that I can, from time to time, bulldoze through decisions without asking my husband what he thinks about it. Independence feels good, but I do recognize that it's helpful to have other opinions in the mix, especially those coming

from someone who genuinely cares about your successes. Gregg is certainly that person in my life.

I'm working on me by . . .

18. **Taking time for me.** Being a celebrity is hard work, that much I can tell you. I might be up at 5 A.M. for a 7 A.M. photo shoot, and then do the show, and then hop a red-eye flight to Los Angeles that arrives in time for another early morning call time, with nothing more than a nap in the car service or on the airplane to sustain me. Some days, I have problems just getting a bite to eat. Mostly, I don't mind the pace. I know that celebrity doesn't last forever, and that if I want to achieve my goals, I have to strike while the iron is hot. But I do recognize that nothing can get done well if my batteries can't be charged. So I'm trying to be better about saying no to unreasonable schedules and demanding a little time for me, even if it's just so that I can sit, take a hot bath, and tune out for a few hours. I find that when I have that little bit of time for myself, I'm much better able to tackle the world.

19. **Dreaming big and embracing my goals fully.** So many opportunities have presented themselves because of my role on *The Real Housewives of Atlanta*, and I'm grateful that I can sift through them and take advantage of all the great things that come with being a reality show star. I'm not content just to be the real girl on the show, though. I want to do much more. And I know that the sky's the limit to what I can achieve, so long as I put my mind to it, whether

to start a boutique hotel (a dream of mine), or to start my own handbag line (a passion of mine), or to have my own TV show. I'm finally in an arena where I can make all sorts of things happen for me, so long as I make the right connections and go big with my ideas. I'm not going to shy away from any of it!

20. **Being grateful and loving myself completely.** There are so many women whom Bravo could have put their mettle behind, so many other girls who would have died for the opportunity I got when I became a part of the cast. Though the work is hard, I remind myself often that this is a fantastic opportunity that I long hoped for. I may not be Janet Jackson, but I am Nene Leakes—reality show star. And I am so happy with the woman I've become.

Acknowledgments

I made a vow when I had my first son that I would raise my children by any means necessary. I credit my children for keeping me humble. I am living a dream and for that I have to thank God for all my blessings. I want to thank: my husband, Gregg, for changing my life and supporting my sons, Bryson and Brentt, and me; my aunt Nena Thomas for always telling me to dream big and it will pay off; my mother's good friend Bessie Freeman for always believing in me. Thanks to my team at Touchstone Fireside who worked on the book and believed that I had a story to tell and a special thanks to my editor, Sulay Hernandez; Victoria Sanders of Victoria Sanders & Associates for pushing to make this happen; my attorney, Darrell Miller; my coauthor, Denene Millner, for her assistance and expertise; and to Bravo Media, True Entertainment, and everyone who worked on the photo shoot for this book cover. Thank you all. I am so grateful!